Michael Leyton

The Structure of
Paintings

Springer Wien New York

Prof. Michael Leyton
Psychology Department, Center for Discrete Mathematics &
Theoretical Computer Science,
Rutgers University, New Brunswick, NJ 08854, USA

E-Mail: mleyton@dimacs.rutgers.edu

© 2006 Springer-Verlag/Wien
Printed in Austria

SpringerWienNewYork is part of
Springer Science+Business Media
springer.com

Cover Illustration: Michael Leyton, *The Supremacy of Line*, New York, 1992,
                    acrylic on canvas, 152 x 122 cm (60 x 48 in)
Typesetting: Camera ready by the author
Printing: Holzhausen Druck und Medien GmbH, 1140 Vienna

Printed on acid-free and chlorine-free bleached paper
SPIN:11784098

With numerous (partly coloured) Figures

Library of Congress Control Number: 2006930614

ISBN-10 3-211-35739-4 SpringerWienNewYork
ISBN-13 978-3-211-35739-2 SpringerWienNewYork

Contents

Chapter 1

Shape as Memory Storage

1.1 Introduction

This is the first in a series of books whose purpose is to give a systematic elaboration of the laws of artistic composition. We shall see that these laws enable us to build up a complete understanding of any painting – both its structure and meaning.

The reason why it is possible to build up such an understanding is as follows. In a series of books and papers, I have developed new foundations to geometry – foundations that are very different from those that have been the basis of geometry for the last 3000 years. A conceptual elaboration of these new foundations was given by my book *Symmetry, Causality, Mind* (MIT Press, 630 pages), and the mathematical foundations were elaborated by my book *A Generative Theory of Shape* (Springer-Verlag, 550 pages). The central proposal of this theory is:

SHAPE = MEMORY STORAGE.

That is: What we mean by shape is memory storage, and what we mean by memory storage is shape.

In the next section, we will see how these new foundations for geometry are directly the opposite of the foundations that have existed from Euclid to modern physics, including Einstein.

My books apply these new foundations to several disciplines: human and computer vision, robotics, software engineering, musical composition, architecture, painting, linguistics, mechanical engineering, computer-aided design and modern physics.

The new foundations unify these disciplines by showing that a result of these foundations is that geometry becomes equivalent to aesthetics. That is, the theory of aesthetics, given by the new foundations, unifies all scientific and artistic disciplines.

Now, as said above, according to the new foundations, shape is equivalent to memory storage. With respect to this, a significant principle of my books is this:

ARTWORKS ARE MAXIMAL MEMORY STORES.

My argument is that the above principle explains the structure and function of artworks. Furthermore, it explains why artworks are the most valuable objects in human history.

1.2   New Foundations to Geometry

This book will show that the new foundations to geometry explain art, whereas the conventional foundations of Euclid and Einstein do not. Thus, to understand art, we need to begin by comparing the two opposing foundations.

The reader was, no doubt, raised to consider Einstein a hero who challenged the basic assumptions of his time. In fact, Einstein's theory of relativity is simply a re-statement of the concept of *congruence* that is basic to Euclid. It is necessary to understand this, and to do so, we begin by considering an example of congruence.

Fig 1.1 shows two triangles. To test if they are congruent, you translate and rotate the upper one to try to make it coincident with the lower one. If exact coincidence is possible, you say that they are *congruent*. This allows you to regard the triangles as essentially the *same object*.

This approach has been the basis of geometry for over 2,000 years, and received its most powerful formulation in the late 19th century by Klein, in the most famous statement in all mathematics – a statement which became the basis not only of all geometry, but of all mathematics and physics: *A geometric object is an invariant (an unchanged property) under some chosen transformations.*

Let us illustrate by returning to the two triangles in Fig 1.1. Consider the upper triangle: It has a number of properties:

(1) Three sides.
(2) Points upward.
(3) Two equal angles.

Now apply a movement to make it coincident with the lower triangle. Properties (1) and (3) remain invariant (unchanged); i.e., the lower triangle also has three sides and has two equal angles. In contrast, property (2) is not invariant; i.e., the triangle no longer points upwards. Klein said that the *geometric* properties are those that remain invariant; i.e., properties (1) and (3).

Now a crucial part of my argument is this: Because properties (1) and (3) are unchanged (invariant) under the movement, *it is impossible to infer from them that the movement has taken place.* Only the non-invariant property, the direction of pointing, allows us to recover the movement. Therefore, in the terminology of my books, I say that *invariants are those properties that are memoryless*; i.e., they yield no information about the past. Because Klein proposes that a geometric object consists of invariants, Klein views geometry as the study of memorylessness.

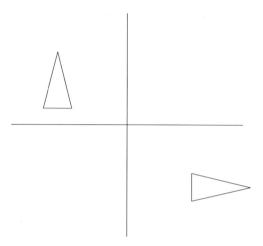

Figure 1.1: Conventional geometry.

Klein's approach became the basis of 20th century mathematics and physics. Thus let us turn to Einstein's theory of relativity. Einstein's fundamental principle says this: The objects of physics are those properties that remain invariant under changes of reference frame. Thus the name "theory of relativity" is the completely wrong name for Einstein's theory. It is, in fact, the theory of *anti-relativity*. It says that one must reject from physics any property that is relative to an observer's reference frame.

Now I argue this: Because Einstein's theory says that the only valid properties of physics are those that do not change in going from one reference frame to another, he is actually implying that physics is the study of those properties from which you cannot recover the fact that there has been a change of reference frame; i.e., they are memoryless to the change of frame.

Einstein's program spread to all branches of physics. For example, quantum mechanics is the study of invariants under the actions of measurement operators. Thus the classification of quantum particles is simply the listing of invariants arising from the energy operator.

The important thing to observe is that this is all simply an application of Klein's theory that geometry is the study of invariants. Notice that Klein's view really originates with Euclid's notion of congruence: The invariants are those properties that allow congruence.

The basis of modern physics can be traced back to Euclid's concern with congruence.

We can therefore say that the entire history of geometry, from Euclid to modern physics, has been founded on the notion of *memorylessness.*

This fundamentally contrasts with the theory of geometry developed in my books. In this theory, a geometric object is a *memory store* for action. Consider the shape of the human body. One can recover from it the history of embryological development and subsequent growth, that the body underwent. The shape is full of its history. There is very little that is congruent between the developed body and the original spherical egg from which it arose. There is very little that has remained invariant from the origin state. I argue that *shape is equivalent to the history that it has undergone*.

Let us therefore contrast the view of geometric objects in the two opposing foundations for geometry:

STANDARD FOUNDATIONS FOR GEOMETRY
(Euclid, Klein, Einstein)
A geometric object is an *invariant;* **i.e.,** *memoryless.*

NEW FOUNDATIONS FOR GEOMETRY
(Leyton)
A geometric object is a *memory store.*

Furthermore, my argument is that the latter view of geometry is the appropriate one for the computational age. A computational system is founded on the use of memory stores. Our age is concerned with the retention of memory rather than the loss of it. We try to buy computers with greater memory, not less. People are worried about declining into old age, because memory decreases.

The point is that, for the computational age, we don't want a theory of geometry based on the notion of memorylessness – the theory of the last 2,500 years. We want a theory of geometry that does the opposite: Equates shape with memory storage. This is the theory proposed and developed in my books.

Furthermore, from this fundamental link between shape and memory storage, I argue the following:

The retrieval of memory from shape is the real meaning of aesthetics.

As a result of this, the new foundations establish the following 3-way equivalence:

Geometry $\equiv$ Memory $\equiv$ Aesthetics.

In fact, my books have shown that this is the basis of artistic composition. The rules by which an artwork is structured are the rules that will enable the artwork to act as a memory store.

The laws of artistic composition are the laws of memory storage.

Let us also consider a simple analogy. A computer has a number of memory stores. They can be inside the computer, or they can be attached as external stores. My claim is that artworks are external memory stores for human beings. In fact, they are the most powerful memory stores that human beings possess.

1.3   The World as Memory Storage

So let us begin. We start by defining memory in the simplest possible way:

Memory   =   Information about the past.

Consequently, we will define a memory store in the following way:

Memory store   =   Any object that yields information about the past.

In fact, I argue that the entire world around us is memory storage, i.e., information about the past. We extract this information from the objects we see. There are many sources of memory. Let us consider some examples. It is worth reading them carefully to fully understand them.

(1) SCARS: A scar on a person's face is, in fact, a memory store. It gives us information about the past: It tells us that, in the past, the surface of the skin was cut. Therefore, past events, i.e., process-history, is stored in a scar.

(2) DENTS: A dent in a car door is also a memory store; i.e., it gives us information about the past: It tells us that, in the past, the door underwent an impact from another object. Therefore, process-history is stored in a dent.

(3) GROWTHS: Any growth is a memory store, i.e., it yields information about the past. For example, the shape of a person's face gives us information that a history of growth has occurred, e.g., the nose and cheekbones grew outward, the wrinkles folded inward, etc. The shape of a tree gives us very accurate information about how it grew. Both, a face and a tree, inform us of a past history. Each is therefore a memory store of process-history.

(4) SCRATCHES: A scratch on a table is information about the past. It informs us that, in the past, the surface had contact with a sharp moving object. Therefore, past events, i.e., process-history, is stored in a scratch.

(5) CRACKS: A crack in a vase is a memory store, i.e., it yields information about the past. It informs us that, in the past, the vase underwent some impact. Therefore, process-history is stored in a crack.

I argue that the world is, in fact, layers and layers of memory storage. One can see this for instance by looking at the relationships between the examples just listed. For example, consider item (1) above, a scar on a person's face. This is memory of scratching. This sits on a person's face, item (3), which is memory of growth. Thus the memory store for scratching – the scar – sits on top of the memory store for growth – the face.

As another example, consider item (5): a crack in a vase. The crack is due to the history of hitting, but the vase on which it occurs is the result of formation from clay on the potter's wheel. Indeed the shape of the vase tells us much about how it was formed. The vertical height is memory of the process that pushed the clay upwards; and the outline of the vase, curving in and out, is memory of the changing pressure of the potter's hands. Therefore the memory store for hitting – the crack – sits on top of the memory store for clay-manipulation – the vase.

According to this theory, therefore, the entire world is memory storage. Each object around us is a memory store of the history of processes that formed it. A central part of my new foundations for geometry is that they establish the rules by which it is possible to extract memory from objects.

1.4   The Fundamental Laws

According to the new foundations, memory storage can take an infinite variety of forms. For example, scars, dents, growths, scratches, twists, cracks, are all memory stores because they all yield information about past actions. However, mathematical arguments given in my books, show that, on a deep level, all memory stores have only one form. This is given by my fundamental laws of memory storage:

FIRST FUNDAMENTAL LAW OF MEMORY STORAGE
(Leyton, 1992)
Memory is stored only in asymmetries.

SECOND FUNDAMENTAL LAW OF MEMORY STORAGE
(Leyton, 1992)
Memory is erased by symmetries.

That is, information about the past can be recovered only from asymmetries. And correspondingly, information about the past is erased by symmetries.

Let us begin with a simple example. Consider the sheet of paper shown on the left in Fig 1.2. Even if one had never seen that sheet before, one would conclude that it had undergone twisting. The reason is that the asymmetry in the sheet yields information about the past. In other words, from the asymmetry, one can *recover* the past history. That is, the *asymmetry acts as a memory store for the past action* – as stated in my First Fundamental Law of Memory Storage (above).

Now let us un-twist the paper, thus obtaining the straight sheet given on the right in Fig 1.2. Suppose we show this straight sheet to any person on the street. Would they be able to infer from it the fact that it had once been twisted? The answer is "No." The reason is that the symmetry of the straight sheet has wiped out the ability to recover the preceding history. This means that the *symmetry erases the memory store* – as stated in my Second Fundamental Law of Memory Storage (above).

Figure 1.2: A twisted sheet is a source of information about the past. A non-twisted sheet is not.

This means that symmetry is the absence of information about the past. In fact, from the symmetry, one concludes that the straight sheet had always been like this. For example, when you take a sheet of paper from a box of paper you have just bought, you do not assume that it had once been twisted or crumpled. Its very straightness (symmetry) leads you to conclude that it had always been straight.

The two diagrams in Fig 1.2 illustrate the two fundamental laws of memory storage given above. These two laws are the very basis of my foundations for geometry. I formulate these two laws in the following way:

LAW 1. ASYMMETRY PRINCIPLE.

An asymmetry in the present is understood as having originated from a past symmetry.

and

LAW 2. SYMMETRY PRINCIPLE.

A symmetry in the present is understood as having always existed.

At first, it might seem as if there are many exceptions to these two laws. In fact, my books show that all the apparent exceptions are due to incorrect descriptions of situations. These laws cannot be violated for deep mathematical reasons.

Now, recall my claim is that artworks are maximal memory stores. My books show:

The Fundamental Laws of Memory Storage = The Fundamental Laws of Art.

We will see that these laws reveal the *complete* structure of any painting. Furthermore, they map out its entire meaning.

Let us now start to develop a familiarity with the two laws. What will be seen, over and over again, is that the way to use the two laws is to go through the following simple procedure: First partition the presented situation into its asymmetries and its symmetries. Then use the Asymmetry Principle (Law 1) on the asymmetries, and the Symmetry Principle (Law 2) on the symmetries. Note that the application of the Asymmetry Principle will return the asymmetries to symmetries. And the application of the Symmetry Principle will preserve the symmetries.

What does one obtain when one applies this procedure to a situation? The answer is this: One obtains the *past*!

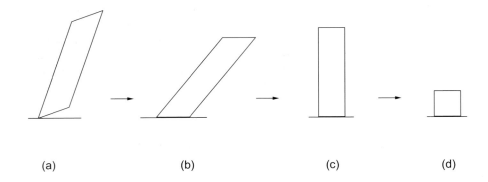

(a)   (b)   (c)   (d)

Figure 1.3: The history inferred from a rotated parallelogram.

Now recall that memory is information about the past, so this procedure is the procedure for the extraction of memory. That is, it converts objects into memory stores.

Since this procedure will be used throughout the book, it will now be stated succinctly as follows:

PROCEDURE FOR RECOVERING THE PAST

(1) Partition the situation into its asymmetries and symmetries.
(2) Apply the Asymmetry Principle to the asymmetries.
(3) Apply the Symmetry Principle to the symmetries.

An extended example will now be considered that will illustrate the power of this procedure, as follows: In a set of psychological experiments that I carried out in the psychology department in Berkeley in 1982, I found that, when subjects are presented with a rotated parallelogram, as shown in Fig 1.3a, they refer it in their heads to a non-rotated parallelogram, Fig 1.3b, which they then refer in their heads to a rectangle, Fig 1.3c, which they then refer in their heads to a square, Fig 1.3d. It is important to understand that the subjects are presented with only the first shape. The rest of the shapes are actually generated by their own minds, as a response to the presented shape.

Close examination reveals that what the subjects are doing is *recovering the history* of the rotated parallelogram. That is, they are saying that, prior to its current state, the rotated parallelogram, Fig 1.3a, was non-rotated, Fig 1.3b, and prior to this it was a rectangle, Fig 1.3c, and prior to this it was a square, Fig 1.3d.

The following should be noted about this sequence. The sequence from *right to left* – that is, going from the square to the rotated parallelogram – represents the direction of *forward time*; i.e., the history starts in the *past* (the square) and ends with the *present* (the rotated parallelogram). Conversely, the sequence from *left to right* – that is, going from the rotated parallelogram to the square – represents the direction of *backward time*. Thus, what the subjects are doing, when their minds generate the sequence of shapes from the rotated parallelogram to square, is this: They are **running time backwards!**

We shall now see that the subjects create this sequence by using the Asymmetry Principle and the Symmetry Principle, i.e., the two above laws for the extraction of memory. Recall that the way one uses the two laws is to apply the simple three-stage Procedure for Recovering the Past, given above: (1) Partition the presented situation into its asymmetries and symmetries, (2) apply the Asymmetry Principle to the asymmetries, and (3) apply the Symmetry Principle to the symmetries.

Thus to use this procedure on the rotated parallelogram, let us begin by identifying the asymmetries in that figure. It is important first to note an important fact:

Asymmetries are the same thing as <u>distinguishabilities</u>.

In the rotated parallelogram, there are three distinguishabilities:

> (1) The distinguishability between the orientation of the shape and the orientation of the environment – indicated by the difference between the bottom edge of the shape and the horizontal line which it touches.

> (2) The distinguishability between adjacent angles in the shape: they are different sizes.

> (3) The distinguishability between adjacent sides in the shape: they are different lengths.

It is clear that what happens in the sequence, from the rotated parallelogram to the square, is that these three distinguishabilities are removed successively backwards in time. The removal of the first distinguishability, that between the orientation of the shape and the orientation of the environment, results in the transition from the rotated parallelogram to the non-rotated one. The removal of the second distinguishability, that between adjacent angles, results in the transition from the non-rotated parallelogram to the rectangle, where the angles are equalized. The removal of the third distinguishability, that between adjacent sides, results in the transition from the rectangle to the square, where the sides are equalized.

Therefore, each successive step in the sequence is a use of the Asymmetry Principle, which says that an asymmetry must be returned to a symmetry backwards in time.

Having identified the asymmetries in the rotated parallelogram and applied the Asymmetry Principle to each of these, we now identify the symmetries in the rotated parallelogram and apply the Symmetry Principle to each of these. First we need an important fact:

Symmetries are the same thing as <u>indistinguishabilities</u>.

In the rotated parallelogram, there are two indistinguishabilities:

> (1) The opposite angles are indistinguishable in size.

> (2) The opposite sides are indistinguishable in length.

The Symmetry Principle requires that these two symmetries in the rotated parallel-ogram must be preserved backwards in time. And indeed, this turns out to be the case. That is, the first symmetry, the equality between opposite angles, in the rotated parallel-ogram, is preserved backwards through the entire sequence: i.e., each subsequent shape, from left to right, has the property that opposite angles are equal. Similarly, the other symmetry, the equality between opposite sides in the rotated parallelogram, is preserved backwards through the entire sequence: i.e., each subsequent shape, from left to right, has the property that opposite sides are equal.

Thus what we have seen in this example is this: The sequence from the rotated parallelogram to the square is determined by two rules: the Asymmetry Principle which returns asymmetries to symmetries, and the Symmetry Principle which preserves the symmetries. These two rules allow us to *recover the past*, i.e., *run time backwards*.

1.5   The Meaning of an Artwork

The preceding section gave what my books have shown are the two Fundamental Laws of Memory Storage, which were also formulated as the Asymmetry Principle and Symmetry Principle. Furthermore, since my claim is that artworks are maximal memory stores, I have also argued that these two laws are *the two most fundamental laws of art*.

According to my foundations for geometry, the history recovered from a memory store is the set of *processes* that produced the current state of the store. The reason is that the foundations constitute a *generative theory*. This is why the book in which I elaborated the mathematical foundations is called *A Generative Theory of Shape* (Springer-Verlag). The idea is that: *shape is defined by the set of processes that produced it*.

Thus, what is being recovered from shape, i.e., from the memory store, is its *process-history*.

According to the new foundations, this gives the *meaning* of an artwork. That is, as argued in my book *Symmetry, Causality, Mind* (MIT Press):

THE MEANING OF AN ARTWORK

The meaning of an artwork is the process-history recovered from it.

We shall see that an important consequence of this is the following: Because the new foundations for geometry allow us to systematically recover the process-history that produced a memory store, we have this:

The new foundations to geometry allow us to systematically map out the entire meaning of an artwork.

1.6   Tension

In this section, the Fundamental Laws of Memory Storage, given in section 1.4, are used to begin a theory of tension in artworks. Any artist knows that an artwork is defined by its structure of tension. Yet remarkably, no one has ever given a theory of tension in artworks. In contrast, this book will give a *complete* theory of tension. The following will be one of the basic proposals made in this book:

TENSION   ≡   MEMORY STORAGE.

The reason why this will be argued is because the following will also be proposed:

Tension is the recovery of the past.

In other words, given the present state, tension is what allows one to recover the past state. Therefore tension must correspond to the rules for the recovery of the past from the present. But the new foundations say that the two fundamental rules for this recovery are the Asymmetry Principle and Symmetry Principle. Therefore, I will now propose the following:

FIRST FUNDAMENTAL LAW OF TENSION.

> **Tension is the use of the Asymmetry Principle. That is, tension occurs from a present asymmetry to its past symmetry.**

To explain: The Asymmetry Principle states that any asymmetry in the present is understood as having arisen from a past symmetry. The above law says that tension is the relation from the present asymmetry to the inferred past symmetry.

The truth of this law will be demonstrated many times in this book. However, as an immediate illustration, let us return to the rotated-parallelogram example of section 1.4. We saw that the rotated parallelogram has three asymmetries, i.e., three distinguishabilities:

> (1) The distinguishability between the orientation of the shape and the orientation of the environment – indicated by the difference between the bottom edge of the shape and the horizontal line which it touches.

> (2) The distinguishability between adjacent angles in the shape: they are different sizes.

> (3) The distinguishability between adjacent sides in the shape: they are different lengths.

The Asymmetry Principle states that each asymmetry is understood as having arisen from a past symmetry. This means that there are exactly three uses of the Asymmetry Principle on the rotated parallelogram, one for each asymmetry.

Now, the First Fundamental Law of Tension, stated above, says that tension is the use of the Asymmetry Principle. This means that there are exactly three types of tension in the rotated parallelogram – one for each use of the Asymmetry Principle. Furthermore, the law allows us to precisely define what these three tensions are. They are:

(1) A tension that tries to reduce the difference between the orientation of the shape and the orientation of the environment; i.e., tries to make the two orientations equal.

(2) A tension that tries to reduce the difference between the sizes of the adjacent angles; i.e., tries to make the sizes of the angles equal.

(3) A tension that tries to reduce the difference between the lengths of the adjacent sides; i.e., tries to make the lengths of the sides the same.

That is, each tension tries to turn a distinguishability into an indistinguishability, i.e., each is an example of returning an asymmetry to symmetry.

Simple as this example is, it illustrates the basic power of the First Fundamental Law of Tension, as follows:

CONSEQUENCE OF THE FIRST FUNDAMENTAL LAW OF TENSION.

There is one tension for each asymmetry. That is, the asymmetries are the sources of tension.

This turns out to be a powerful tool in the analysis of artistic composition, as follows:

CONSEQUENCE OF THE FIRST FUNDAMENTAL LAW OF TENSION.

The First Fundamental Law allows one to systematically elaborate all the tensions in a figure; i.e., elaborate the asymmetries and establish their symmetrizations.

The law will be illustrated many times in the book.

1.7   Tension in Curvature

The ideas developed in the previous sections will now be used to carry out an analysis of what I will argue is one of the major forms of tension in an artwork: *curvature*. We shall see that this gives enormous insight into artistic composition.

Let us state precisely what the goal will be: In accord with the theory of this book – i.e., that art is memory storage – we will develop a theory of how *history is recovered from curved shapes*. Since this is the history of past *processes* that produced the present shape, we will refer to it as *process-history*. It will be seen that the recovered process-history will yield the *tension* structure of such shapes.

The next few sections will be concerned with closed smooth shapes such as that shown in Fig 1.4. The shape is *closed*, in that it does not have any ends; and it is *smooth*, in that it does not have any sharp corners. Later on, the techniques developed for such shapes will be generalized to arbitrary shapes.

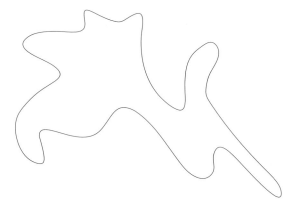

Figure 1.4: A closed smooth curve.

Our concern will be to solve the following problem: When presented with a shape like Fig 1.4, how can one infer the preceding history that produced that shape? In other words, we will be trying to solve what my books call the **history-recovery problem** for that shape.

1.8 Curvature Extrema

We now begin an analysis of how curvature creates tension in an artwork. First, it is necessary to understand the meaning of *curvature*. In the case of curves in the two-dimensional plane, curvature is easy to define. Quite simply, curvature is the *amount of bend*.

Thus, consider the downward sequence of lines shown in Fig 1.5. The line at the top has no bend. Therefore one says that it has zero curvature. The next line downwards has more bend, and thus one says that it has more curvature. The line below this has even more bend, and so one says that it has even more curvature.

Now, the curve at the bottom of Fig 1.5, should be examined carefully. It exhibits a property that is going to be crucial to the entire discussion. The property is this: There is a point, shown as E on the curve, that has more curvature (bend) than the other points on the curve. Let us examine this more closely:

There is a simple way to judge how much curvature there is at some point of a curve. Imagine that you are driving a car along a road shaped exactly like the curve. The amount of curvature at any point on the road is the amount that *the steering wheel is turned*. Obviously, for a sharp bend in the road, the steering wheel must be turned a considerable amount. This is because a sharp bend has a lot of curvature. In contrast, for a straight section of road, the steering wheel should not be turned at all; it should point directly ahead. This is because a straight section of road has no curvature.

Let us now return to the bottom curve shown in Fig 1.5. If one drives around this

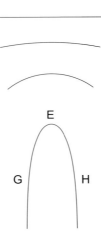

Figure 1.5: Successively increasing curvature.

curve, it is clear that, at point E, the wheel would have to be turned a considerable amount: That is, point E involves a sharp bend in the road.

However, contrast this with driving through point G shown on the curve. The wheel, in this region, should remain relatively straight, because the road there involves almost no bend, i.e., no curvature. The same applies to point H on the other side.

Thus, let us try to see what happens when one drives along the entire curve. Suppose one starts at the left end. Initially, the steering wheel is straight for quite a while. But then, as one gets closer to E, one must start turning the wheel, until at E, the amount of turn reaches a *maximum*. After one passes through E, however, one slowly begins to straighten the wheel again. And, in the final part of the road, the wheel becomes almost straight.

Because point E has the extreme amount of curvature, it is called a **curvature extremum**. Curvature extrema are going to be very important in the following discussion. We shall see that their role in an artwork is crucial.

1.9   Symmetry in Complex Shape

Since every aspect of the theory will be founded on the notion of symmetry, it is necessary to look at how symmetry is defined in a complex shape. In particular, one must understand how reflectional symmetry is defined in complex shape, as follows:

Defining reflectional symmetry on a simple shape is easy. Consider the triangle show in Fig 1.6. It is a simple shape. One establishes symmetry in this shape merely by placing a mirror on the shape, in such a position that it reflects one half of the figure onto the other. The line, along which the mirror lies, is called the symmetry axis. It is shown as the vertical dashed line in the figure.

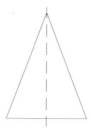

Figure 1.6: A simple shape having a straight mirror symmetry.

In contrast, consider a complex shape like that shown earlier in Fig 1.4 (p13). We cannot place a mirror on it so that it will reflect one half onto the other. Nevertheless, we shall see now that such a shape does contain a very subtle form of reflectional symmetry, and this is central to the way the mind defines the structure of tension in the figure.

Consider the two curves, c_1 and c_2, shown in Fig 1.7. The goal is to find the symmetry axis between the two curves. Observe that one cannot take a mirror and reflect one curve onto the other. For example, the top curve shown is more curved than the bottom one. Therefore a mirror will not send the top one onto the bottom one.

The way one proceeds is as follows: Insert a circle between the two curves as shown in Fig 1.8. It must touch the two curves simultaneously. For example, in this figure, we see the circle touching the upper curve at A, while simultaneously touching the lower curve at B.

Next, drag the circle along the two curves, always making sure that the circle touches the upper and lower curve simultaneously. As can be seen, one might have to expand or contract the circle so that it can touch the two curves at the same time.

Finally, as the circle moves, keep track of a particular point, Q, shown in Fig 1.8. This point is on the circle, half way between the two touch points A and B. As the circle moves along the two curves, it leaves a trajectory of points Q. This trajectory is indicated by the dotted line. The dotted line is then called the *symmetry axis* between the two curves.

Comment: For those who are familiar with symmetry axes based on the circle, one should note that the axis of Blum [1] was based on the circle center, the axis of Brady [2] was based on the chord midpoint between A and B, and the axis described above is based on the arc midpoint between A and B. This last analysis was invented by me in Leyton [16] and has particular topological properties that make it highly suitable for the inference of process-history. I therefore called it *Process-Inferring Symmetry Analysis (PISA).* [1]

---

[1] In fact, the full definition of PISA involves extra conditions discussed in my previous books.

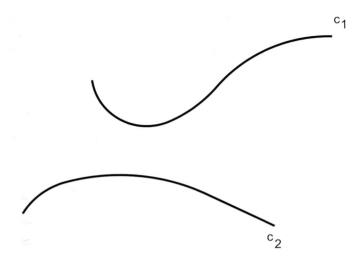

Figure 1.7: How can one construct a symmetry axis between these to curves?

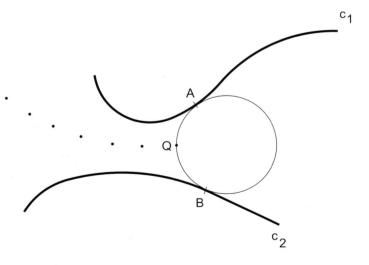

Figure 1.8: The points Q define the symmetry axis.

1.10   Symmetry-Curvature Duality

The previous section defined the symmetry axis for arbitrary smooth curves. The section preceding that considered curvature extrema. Curvature extrema and symmetry axes are two entirely different structural aspects of a shape. A curvature extremum is a point lying *on* a curve. In contrast, not only does a symmetry axis lie *off* a curve, it is in fact a relation *between* two curves.

Given the very different nature of curvature extrema and symmetry axes, mathematicians did not previously suspect that there was a relationship between the two. However, in the 1980s, I proved a theorem which shows that there is an extremely strong relationship between them – in fact, a duality. I called the theorem, the Symmetry-Curvature Duality Theorem. Since I published the theorem, it has been applied by scientists in over 40 disciplines, from DNA tracking to chemical engineering:

SYMMETRY-CURVATURE DUALITY THEOREM.
Leyton (1987)

Any section of smooth curve, with one and only one curvature extremum, has one and only one symmetry axis. This axis is forced to terminate at the extremum itself.

To illustrate this theorem, consider the curve shown in Fig 1.9. It is part of a much larger curve. The part shown here has three curvature extrema labeled sequentially: m_1, M, and m_2.

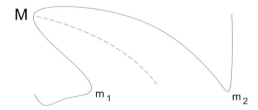

Figure 1.9: Illustration of the Symmetry-Curvature Duality Theorem.

Now, consider only the section of curve *between* the two extrema m_1 and m_2. This section is shaped like a *wave*. Most crucially, it has only *one* curvature extremum, M.

The question to be asked is this: How many symmetry axes does this section of curve possess? The above theorem gives us the answer. It says: Any section of curve with only one curvature extremum has only one symmetry axis. Thus we conclude that the section of curve containing only the extremum M can have only one axis.

The next question to be asked is this: Where does this symmetry axis go? Could it, for example hit the upper side or lower side of the wave? Again, the theorem provides us with the answer. It says that the axis is forced to terminate at the tip of the wave, i.e., the extremum M itself – as shown in Fig 1.9.

This theorem is enormously valuable in understanding the structure of any complex curve: Simply break down the curve into sections, each with only one curvature extremum. The theorem then tells us that each of these sections has only one symmetry axis, and that the axis terminates at the extremum.

Fig 1.10 illustrates this decompositional procedure. The curve has sixteen extrema. Thus, the theorem says that there must be sixteen symmetry axes associated with and terminating at those extrema. These axes are shown as the dashed lines on the figure.

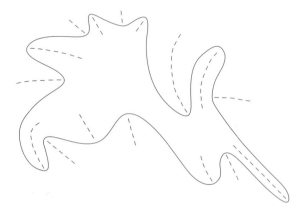

Figure 1.10: Sixteen extrema imply sixteen symmetry axes.

1.11   Curvature Extrema and the Symmetry Principle

Recall that the problem we are trying to solve is this: When presented with a shape like Fig 1.10, how can one convert it into a memory store, i.e., recover from it the process-history that produced it. Section 1.4 gave my two fundamental laws of memory storage, i.e., for the recovery of process-history from shape. These laws are the Asymmetry Principle, which states that any asymmetry in the present shape is assumed to have arisen from a past symmetry; and the Symmetry Principle, which states that any symmetry in the present shape is assumed to have always existed. Both principles must be applied to the shape. Let us first use the Symmetry Principle.

The Symmetry Principle demands that one must preserve symmetries in the shape, backwards in time. What are the symmetries? The previous section established significant symmetries in the shape: the symmetry axes illustrated in Fig 1.10, predicted by the Symmetry-Curvature Duality Theorem: i.e., those axes corresponding to the curvature extrema.

Now use the Symmetry Principle, which states that any symmetry must be preserved backward in time. In particular, it demands that the symmetry axes must be preserved backwards in time.

There is, in fact, only one way that this preservation of axes can be accomplished: As one runs time backwards, the past processes must move backwards along the axes. However, this means that, in the forward-time direction, the processes must have moved along the axes. Thus we conclude:

INTERACTION PRINCIPLE.

The symmetry axes are the directions along which processes are most likely to have acted.

This rule becomes particularly significant when combined with the considerations of the next section.

1.12 Curvature Extrema and the Asymmetry Principle

According to my foundations to geometry, the recovery of process-history from shape requires that one apply both the Symmetry Principle and the Asymmetry Principle. The previous section applied the Symmetry Principle. The present section applies the Asymmetry Principle.

The Asymmetry Principle states that an asymmetry in the present is understood as having arisen from a past symmetry. It is now necessary to fully define the asymmetry which will be the concern for the remainder of this volume. To understand it, let us look at a shape such as the human hand, shown in Fig 1.11. We will imagine that we are driving along a road which has exactly this shape. The purpose is to examine the curvature at different points along the road. Recall that the curvature, at any point, is given by the amount that a car steering wheel is turned at that point. Thus, if the steering wheel is directed straight ahead, at some point, then there is no curvature (bend) at that point. However, if the steering wheel is turned a large amount, at some point, then there is a large amount of curvature at that point.

Let us start with the point A on the outer side of the little finger. The curve at this point is relatively straight, i.e., it has little bend. The steering wheel would be pointing almost straight ahead here. Therefore, there would be almost no bend at A, that is, almost no curvature.

Now continue driving up the finger to the point B on the tip. It is clear that, at B, the wheel would now be turned quite far. Thus, the road has a lot of curvature at B.

Let us now drive further along the finger, reaching point C. Here, the steering wheel points almost straight ahead, because the curve has straightened out again. Thus, there is almost no bend in the curve at C, that is, almost no curvature.

Now continue to point D in the dip between the fingers. The steering wheel must be turned considerably at D, and therefore there is considerable curvature here.

The reader can now see what will happen if we continue to drive along the curve. The curvature will be almost zero along the side of the next finger, it will become very large as we move around the tip of that finger, it will become almost zero again as we travel down the other side of that finger, it will become very large in the next dip, and so on.....

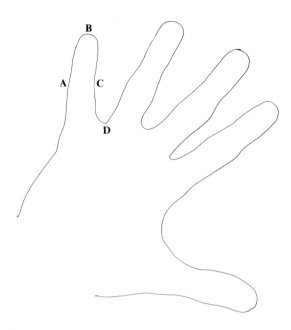

Figure 1.11: The curvature is different at different points around the curve.

The conclusion therefore is that *curvature changes as one moves around the curve*. This means that curvature is different at different points of the curve – that is, it is *distinguishable* at different points on the curve.

CURVATURE DISTINGUISHABILITY

> **On a typical curve, the curvature (amount of bend) is different at different points.**

Now, recall that distinguishability is the same thing as *asymmetry*. In fact, the distinguishability in curvature, around the curve, is the asymmetry which will concern us for the remainder of this volume (the later volumes will examine other asymmetries). We will systematically elaborate the rules of art with respect to this asymmetry, and see that this gives enormous insight into the structure of paintings.

CURVATURE ASYMMETRY

> **For the rest of this volume, the asymmetry being considered is curvature distinguishability; i.e., the differences in curvature at the different points around the curve.**

Let us now see what happens when one applies the Asymmetry Principle to this distinguishability. The principle says that any distinguishability in the present must go back to indistinguishability in the past. This means that the differences in curvature on the shape must be removed backwards in time, leaving a shape in which curvature is the same (indistinguishable) at all points around it.

There is, in fact, only one smooth closed shape in which curvature is the same at all points. It is the circle. The conclusion from this is that *the past of any smooth closed shape is a circle*.

Consider an example. We have been looking at the outline of a hand. This curve is part of a closed smooth shape: the outline of the entire body. Now, it is a remarkable fact that the past of the body is a circle: The body grows from a circular egg.

The extraordinary thing is that one need know nothing about biology to arrive at this conclusion. The Asymmetry Principle gives us this conclusion immediately. The Asymmetry Principle removes the need for a biological science. It is a basic argument of my books that the different laws of the different sciences can be replaced by a single set of memory laws – the general rules for recovering the past from shape.

1.13   General Shapes

So far, the rules have been applied to smooth, closed curves. However, the rules apply equally to any type of curve – e.g., those that contain sharp corners or are not closed. As I have shown in my previous books, the past of any curve is either a (1) circle, (2) straight line or (3) regular polygon. Notice that, like a circle, a straight line has the same curvature at each point (in fact, the curvature is zero at each point). Notice also that, except at the corners, a polygon is straight everywhere, and therefore also has constant curvature at each point. Constant curvature is a basic symmetry of past shapes.

1.14   The Three Rules

Let us now put together the rules established in the preceding sections, for recovering process-history from closed smooth shapes; i.e., *converting the shapes into memory stores*. There are a total of three rules, as follows.

Rule 1.
This is the Symmetry-Curvature Duality Theorem. It says that, to each curvature extremum, there is a unique symmetry axis leading to, and terminating at, the extremum.

What this theorem does for us is the following: Suppose one is presented, in an artwork, with a curved line such as that shown in Fig 1.12. Then the first thing one does is pick out the curvature extrema. The theorem then says that each curvature extremum implies a symmetry axis leading to the extremum. Therefore, the use of this rule inserts symmetry axes into the shape, thus producing the diagram given in Fig 1.13.

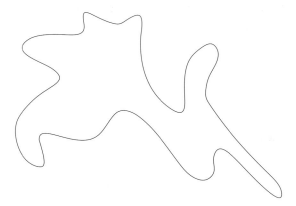

Figure 1.12: A closed smooth shape.

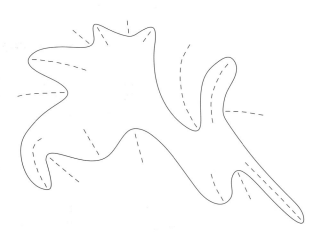

Figure 1.13: The inferred axes.

Rule 2.
The second rule is the Symmetry Principle, which states that symmetries must be pre-served backwards in time. This means, in particular, that any symmetry axis must be preserved in the conjectured process-history. One preserves an axis, maximally, by making sure that the conjectured process went along the axis. Thus our second rule is a specific example of the Symmetry Principle. This rule, called the Interaction Principle, states that the historical processes went along the symmetry axes.

Rule 3.
The final rule is the Asymmetry Principle, which states that any asymmetry in the present is understood as having originated from a past symmetry. The asymmetry being considered is the difference in curvature at the different points around the curve. The Asymmetry Principle implies that this difference must be removed backwards in time. Thus the past is a curve that has the same curvature at each point.

1.15   Process Diagrams

Together, the three rules imply that a curved shape was created by processes that pushed the boundary along the axes. For example, the protrusions, in Fig 1.13, were created by pushing the boundary out along the axes, and the indentations were created by pushing the boundary in along the axes. In fact, the processes actually created the curvature extrema. This is a crucial conclusion from the above rules. The original curve, in the past, had no extrema. This is because the original curve had equal curvature at all points, i.e., no extremes! Thus we conclude:

> **Each process went along a symmetry axis and created the extremum at the end of the axis.**

The processes will be represented by putting arrows along the axes, as illustrated in Fig 1.14. The arrows lead to the extrema, and indicate that the extrema were created by the processes. A diagram like this will be called a **process diagram.**

1.16   Trying out the Rules

To demonstrate the power of the three rules, they will now be tested on a large catalogue of shapes: all shapes with up to, and including, eight curvature extrema. The catalogue provides *purely the outlines* exhibited in Fig 1.15, 1.16, and 1.17.[2] What I have done is taken these outlines and applied to them the above three rules for the recovery of process-history. The result is given by the arrows on each shape. As the reader can see, the inferred histories accord exactly with our intuitive sense of how these shapes were formed. These results will be examined in considerable detail in the next chapter.

---

[2]Most of these outlines come from a paper by Richards, Koenderink & Hoffman [24].

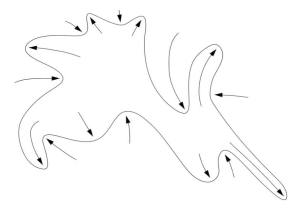

Figure 1.14: The processes inferred by the rules.

1.17   How the Rules Conform to the Procedure for Recovering the Past

The three rules clearly illustrate the simple three-part procedure given in section 1.4 for recovering the past. The procedure was this:

PROCEDURE FOR RECOVERING THE PAST.

(1) Partition the situation into its asymmetries and symmetries.
(2) Apply the Asymmetry Principle to the asymmetries.
(3) Apply the Symmetry Principle to the symmetries.

The correspondence between the three rules and the three parts of the procedure is this: Recall that Rule 1 is the Symmetry-Curvature Duality Theorem, which states that, to each curvature extremum, there is a symmetry axis leading to the extremum. This rule, in fact, corresponds to part 1 of the above procedure: It is the partitioning of the shape into asymmetries and symmetries. The particular asymmetries it chooses are the curvature extrema; and the particular symmetries it chooses are the symmetry axes. The theorem describes a partitioning of the shape into asymmetries and symmetries, in this way: It states that, for each unit of asymmetry – i.e., each curvature extremum – there is a unit of symmetry – i.e., a symmetry axis. This completely partitions the shape into asymmetries and symmetries.

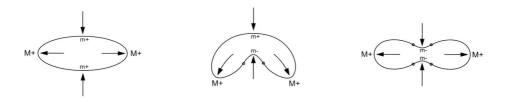

Figure 1.15: The inferred histories on the shapes with 4 extrema.

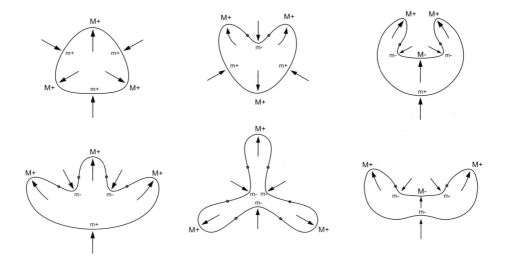

Figure 1.16: The inferred histories on the shapes with 6 extrema.

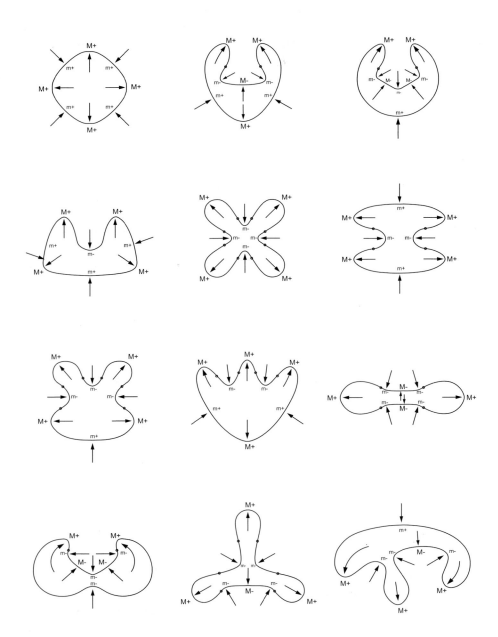

Figure 1.17: The inferred histories on the shapes with 8 extrema.

Now let us turn to Rules 2 and 3. As stated in section 1.14, these two rules are particular uses of the Symmetry Principle and Asymmetry Principle, respectively. Thus Rules 2 and 3 correspond respectively to parts 3 and 2 of the above procedure. It does not matter that the order of the two parts is reversed, since the Asymmetry Principle and Symmetry Principle are in fact always used simultaneously, because they together create the backward recovery of time.

1.18   Applying the Rules to Artworks

Let us now apply the three rules to artworks, and show that the rules reveal crucial aspects of the tension structure. Recall that my First Fundamental Law of Tension (p11) states that tension is the use of the Asymmetry Principle. Since, the Asymmetry Principle occurs as one of the three process rules, I conclude that the **inferred process-structure corresponds to the tension structure**. This will be strongly supported in the following case-studies. For reference during the case studies, the three rules are stated here succinctly:

> **(1) Symmetry-Curvature Duality Theorem.**
> *Each curvature extremum has a unique axis leading to, and terminating at, the extremum.*

> **(2) Symmetry Principle applied to symmetry axes.**
> *The processes, which created the shape, went along symmetry axes.*

> **(3) Asymmetry Principle applied to curvature variation.**
> *Differences in curvature must be removed backwards in time.*

1.19   Case Studies

1.19.1   Picasso: *Large Still-Life with a Pedestal Table*

Since Picasso has some of the most advanced use of line in the history of art, this inevitably means that his central tool is the use of curvature extrema. Consider his *Large Still-Life on a Pedestal Table*, shown in color in Plate 1.

Picasso builds up tension by creating continual differences in curvature along curves. This is achieved in accord with the rules given above. To see this, consider Fig 1.18, which shows the result of applying the rules: First, the curvature extrema were located. Then the symmetry axes leading to the extrema were established. And finally, for each axis, an arrow was drawn consisting merely of the symmetry axis itself, together with an arrow-head placed at the extremum. The resulting process diagram clearly captures major aspects of the tension structure.

Figure 1.18: Curvature extrema and their inferred processes in Picasso's *Still-Life*.

Most crucially, the figure shows the painting as essentially a *memory store*. **The artist loads actions into the shape-structure and the process of experiencing the work is the process of retrieving those actions.**

1.19.2 Raphael: *Alba Madonna*

Next turn to Raphael's *Alba Madonna*, shown in Plate 2. We shall see that this painting is structurally a set of powerful well-defined foci linked by strong movements connecting the foci centers. Our three rules are highly significant in setting up this structure.

First consider the two foci, shown in Fig 1.19a and b. The left one is at the ear of the left-most child (John the Baptist), and the right one is at the elbow of the Madonna. Between these two foci, there is an enormous tension, that can be experienced by looking at the actual painting, Plate 2. This tension is created by the three rules, as follows. First observe that each of these two foci occur at a strongly-defined curvature extremum:

(1) The first extremum is at the child's ear, and is shown in Fig 1.20. By comparing this figure with the actual painting, Plate 2, one can see how carefully Raphael defines this extremum. The upper side of the extremum is the line of the Madonna's arm which descends diagonally down to the ear. The lower side of the extremum is the line that descends from the ear along the shoulder of the child, through its hand, and ends at the Madonna's knee.

(2) The other extremum is the elbow of the Madonna, on the right – which of course faces rightward.

By the Symmetry-Curvature Duality Theorem, these two extrema each have a symmetry axis. In fact, Raphael ensures that they share the same symmetry axis – which is the horizontal line linking the two extrema. Raphael strongly emphasizes this line by presenting it as the highlighted *waist-line* of the Madonna – see the painting, Plate 2.

Now, since our rules dictate that there must be a process running along any symmetry axis leading to an extremum, we must have an arrow pointing along the axis to the child's ear on the left, and an arrow pointing in the opposite direction along the axis to the Madonna's elbow on the right. These two arrows *pull the extrema apart* and are responsible for the considerable tension that exists between the two extrema.

Notice that the artist adds even further dynamics to the horizontal axis, again by using the three rules. For example, in the waist of the Madonna, there is a sharp left-ward pointing arrow-head of clothing terminating at the left end of the waist-line, as shown in Fig 1.21. The reader should find this arrow-head in the actual painting, Plate 2. Its lower edge is the lower edge of the red shirt; its upper edge is the diagonal fold that

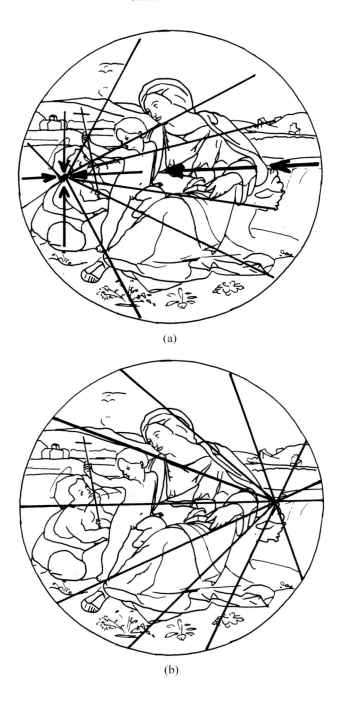

(a)

(b)

Figure 1.19: A focus on (a) the left and (b) the right, in Raphael's *Alba Madonna*.

Figure 1.20: Curvature extremum at the ear in Raphael's *Alba Madonna*.

Figure 1.21: Significant arrow in the clothing in Raphael's *Alba Madonna*.

descends in the red shirt to the left end of the waist. Its approximate symmetry axis is the horizontal waist-line.

This arrow-head defines a leftward movement on the waist, and reinforces the movement towards the child's ear on the left. Notice also that this arrow-head in the waist occurs exactly under the Madonna's face, and emphasizes the leftward direction of her gaze.

One can see therefore how carefully Raphael sets up the dynamics in the painting, via our three rules. But this is only the beginning, as follows:

Let us turn to one of the other main foci of the painting: the powerful one at the Madonna's foot – Fig 1.22. This occurs where the Madonna's ankle touches the toe of Christ (the child in the center).

What should be observed now is that this focus is constructed entirely by curvature extrema. Each arrow shown in Fig 1.22 is a symmetry axis leading to an extremum at the tip of the arrow, in accord with our three rules. To appreciate the enormous subtlety with which Raphael uses these rules to set up the focus, it is worthwhile examining the curvature extrema in detail, as follows:

Turn to the actual painting, Plate 2. Consider first the red piece of clothing that lies on the ground to the right of the focus. It is literally an arrow-head that points directly into the focus. In fact, it has exactly the same shape and size as the arrow-head in the waist of the Madonna. Whereas the latter pointed towards the focus at the child's ear, this one points at the focus in the Madonna's ankle. It does so, of course, in accord with our three rules; i.e., it has a symmetry axis leading into its vertex, a sharp curvature extremum. The focus, at the ankle, then lies along the line established by the symmetry axis in this arrow-head.

Now observe that, directly opposite this arrow-head, on the other side of the ankle-focus, there is the leg of the *kneeling child* (John the Baptist). The knee itself is a curvature extremum. Thus, in accord with the Symmetry-Curvature Duality Theorem, it has a symmetry axis leading to the extremum. This symmetry axis is, in fact, the axis of the entire visible portion of the leg. Correspondingly, there is a process-arrow leading to the extremum. Note that it points directly to the focus point in the Madonna's ankle.

Raphael therefore sets up the following structure: The arrow in the leg and the arrow in the isolated red triangle on the opposite side of the ankle-focus are *exactly the same distance from the focus center*. Furthermore, they lie along the same line. Visually, they *exactly balance each other*, and provide a powerful inward pull into the focus.

Next observe that this pair of arrows is divided *vertically in two* by the straight vertical leg of the Christ child, which plunges down to the Madonna's foot. The symmetry axis of the Christ's leg is a long line that terminates downward at the curvature extremum defined by the curved shadow line in the child's ankle. Note that, above the child's hip, this line is further reinforced by becoming the edge-line of the child's torso. This is a technique that is often used in art: defining a line that changes from being a symmetry axis to an edge-line, and vice versa.

Now, let us take the perpendicular angle between the vertical leg and the red arrow-head on the ground. This angle is itself divided into two halves by the *Madonna's* leg, which descends diagonally. The light area down her leg is a demarcated independent area in its own right – by virtue of its lightness and the creases in the clothing.

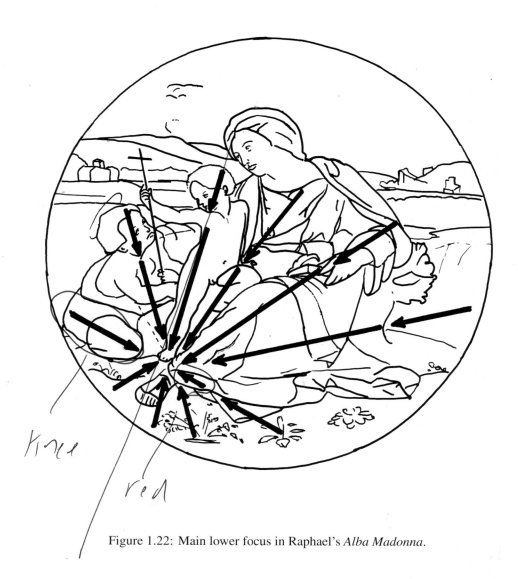

Figure 1.22: Main lower focus in Raphael's *Alba Madonna*.

This light area possesses a symmetry axis, which descends diagonally and terminates at the curvature extremum defined by the crease in the Madonna's clothing at her ankle. The associated arrow is shown in Fig 1.22, as the arrow descending through her knee.

Now, returning to Plate 2, one can see that this light area, and the vertical leg of Christ, together enclose a dark area which constitutes another sharp arrow-head, that descends powerfully down to the Madonna's ankle.

This dark area is matched by a dark area between the Madonna's diagonal leg and the ground, and this latter dark area also defines a curvature extremum into the Madonna's ankle.

Therefore, an alternation of dark and light curvature extrema occurs all the way around the focal point, as alternating positive and negative space, each having a symmetry axis leading to an extremum. For example, the Madonna's foot defines an upward-pointing light extremum at the ankle, and has a dark area of ground on either side – each dark area also defining its own curvature extremum into the ankle.

1.19.3   Cézanne: *Italian Girl Resting on Her Elbow*

Let us now turn to a very different type of painting: Cézanne's *Italian Girl Resting on Her Elbow*, known more recently as *Young Italian Woman at a Table*, shown in Plate 3.

Fig 1.23 shows several of the significant movements of the painting, all inferred by the three rules, i.e., all lying along symmetry axes leading to curvature extrema. The figure therefore shows the painting as a *memory store* of those movements.

In order to more deeply understand the structure of this painting, let us return to Plate 3. Observe first that the painting is largely driven by horn-like structures. Most prominent of these is the massive central scarf that pulls down from the girl's face to her waist. In addition, one has the white horn that starts from the middle of the left edge, and leads one's eye from this edge to her elbow. Also significant is the horn created by her lower hand on the table, and the opposing dark horn that leads from the lower left edge to her hand. Various horns also swirl around her elbow, and, in addition, form the edge of her back. Together, this entire set of horns creates a complex structure of movements and counter-movements across the canvas. All of these movements are inferred by our three rules, i.e., they are processes lying along symmetry axes leading to curvature extrema.

An additional major theme is that of pointing triangles. These pull the table-cloth in various opposing directions. Furthermore, they make up the girl's dark skirt, and of course the large white sleeve above the skirt. Again, these movements are inferred by our three rules – they are processes along symmetry axes leading to extrema.

Now, let us turn to the crucial role of the arm, on which her face rests. In fact, this factor is so significant that it is referred to in the most frequent title of the painting, *Italian Girl Resting on Her Elbow*. The "elbow" referred to in the title is in fact a *curvature extremum*. The axis leading to the extremum is the symmetry axis between the two long edges of the fore-arm. These two edges actually continue up into the face becoming her mouth and her eyes. The axis itself is continued in the nose. Each of these latter elements – the eyes, the mouth, and the nose – have the horn shape described earlier, showing the enormous integration of the work. Notice, for example, how the pouting

Figure 1.23: Forces leading to curvature extrema in Cézanne's *Italian Girl*.

mouth is echoed in each of the horns described earlier, e.g, the horn on her shoulder, and the vertical horn on the left of her elbow.

Now, as was said, the two edges of the arm are continued in the face. Thus the movement down the arm actually starts in the face. In this way, Cezanne pulls the strong psychological content of the face into the movement along the arm axis.

Now observe that, as shown in Fig 1.23, this movement down the arm is contravened by two lateral movements, one along the main axis of the head, and the other in the hand that supports the head. These lateral movements are set up by curvature extrema, as shown. By opposing the movement down the arm, this dynamic gives the face a sense of weight and resistance against the downward pull of the arm.

In addition, there is an important curvature extremum at the ear, where the jaw-line meets the hair-line. The resulting arrow is also shown in Fig 1.23.

The arm and face structure can now be put together. The axis of the arm extends from the elbow not only up the entire arm but across the entire face to the ear. At the elbow, this axis has a downward pointing extremum. At the ear, it has an upward pointing extremum. These two opposing movements pull subtly against each other. Contradicting them, and slicing through them, are the main axis of the face, from fore-head to chin, and the axes in the fingers.

All these movements are produced simply by the three rules given earlier.

1.19.4   de Kooning: *Black Painting*

The next painting is by de Kooning, shown in Plate 4. It is one of the *Black Paintings* of 1948. The structure of this work is so complex that I will build it up, step by step.

First observe that it is constructed of shapes of the type given in Fig 1.24. The three shown in this figure are drawn in exactly the positions they occur in the painting – they all happen to be black. The arrows are those produced by our three rules. It is clear that they again capture the dynamics of the shapes.

Next observe that the canvas is a *mosaic* of such shapes; i.e., they are *fitted together* across the canvas. For example, Fig 1.25 shows some more shapes from the painting. Observe, for instance, that the lowest upward arrow (just left and below the center of Fig 1.25), fits exactly between two of the shapes in the previous figure (Fig 1.24). It is worthwhile seeing this in the actual painting (Plate 4).

Because each of these shapes has its own dynamic, and because the painting consists of such shapes fitted together, the entire canvas possesses a fluid quality, i.e., every part of the painting is alive with such movement.

In fact, this movement occurs on several levels of size, as will now be seen. Consider first Fig 1.26. It shows some of the important white structure. Again, the dynamics inferred by our three rules have been indicated, i.e., all the arrows are processes along symmetry axes leading to curvature extrema.

However, observe now that, on a higher level of scale, one can consider the white structure as a single large mass shown by the *unbroken* outline in Fig 1.26. The *broken* lines merely indicate the positions of the black masses within the *overall* white mass.

Figure 1.24: Inferred processes from curvature extrema in one of de Kooning's *Black Paintings*.

Figure 1.25: More inferred processes from curvature extrema (de Kooning *Black Painting*).

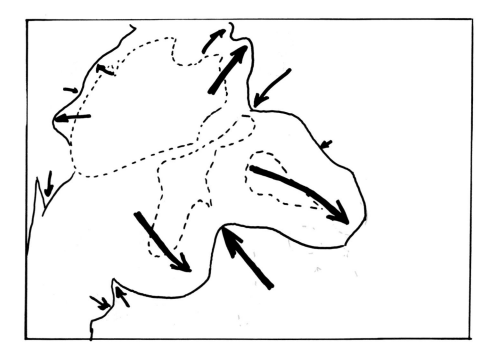

Figure 1.26: Still more inferred processes from curvature extrema (de Kooning *Black Painting*).

Nevertheless, it is clear, when looking at the painting, that the white mass can be viewed as a single cohesive shape, whose border is the *unbroken* line in Fig 1.26.

Now, this large mass has a dynamic structure. Again, this structure is given simply by applying our three rules. That is, the arrows shown in Fig 1.26 are the inferred processes along symmetry axes leading to extrema.

The crucial thing to observe is that these arrows lie over the arrows in the previous diagram, Fig 1.25. The arrows of the previous diagram give the dynamics of the individual separate masses, whereas the arrows in the present diagram give the dynamics of the white mass as a whole. The two diagrams show different flows in the work, and these flows lie on top of each other.

Now let us take all the diagrams we have produced so far, together with the dynamics of a couple more shapes, and simply superimpose them all on one diagram. The result is Fig 1.27. This gives a remarkably strong sense of the structure of the painting. Remember: all that we have done is to apply the three rules to the shapes, and simply superimpose the results.

On this diagram, one can see examples of arrows lying over each other in different directions because the previous figures gave two systems of arrows over the same region.

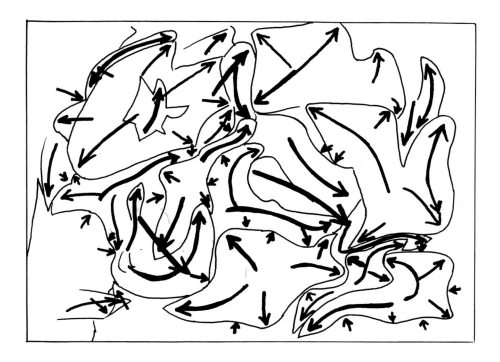

Figure 1.27: Layers of tension (de Kooning *Black Painting*).

I will call this effect *layered tension*, and propose that it is a fundamentally important phenomenon in art.

LAYERED TENSION

Layered tension is the superimposition of levels of tension over the same region.

I shall often use the term "thickening" in connection with the phenomenon of layered tension, as follows:

THICKENING

When layered tension has been created over a region, we shall say that tension has been thickened over that region.

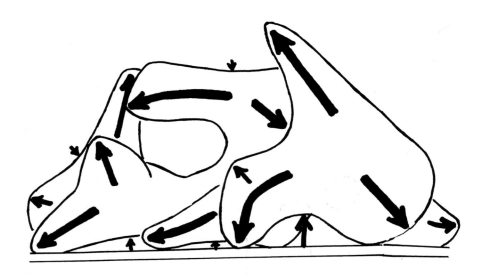

Figure 1.28: Curvature extrema and their inferred processes in Henry Moore's *Three Piece #3, Vertebrae*).

1.19.5   Henry Moore: *Three Piece #3, Vertebrae*

In order to show the reader that the three curvature rules apply not just to painting, the final example chosen in this section is a *sculpture*. It is Henry Moore's *Three Piece #3, Vertebrae*, see Fig 1.28.

This figure shows what happens when the three rules are applied to the sculpture. That is, the arrows shown are the processes leading along symmetry axes to curvature extrema. Clearly, the rules capture the dynamics of the sculpture very powerfully.

The work consists of a strong upward diagonal extremum on the right. This is then understood as bent over to become the horizontal piece in the top middle section of the work. Finally, it is seen as turned around along the opposite diagonal, as the upward extremum at the top left.

Similarly, a sequence of three extrema define the bottom of the work, each one being a limb that projects downward to touch the ground. Notice that these three downward extrema contrast with a sequence of three *upward* extrema, *also along the bottom*, rising gently from the base.

Finally, observe that, all around the work, the artist has carefully pushed the outline inward and outward with small-scale extrema that modulate the outline and add a further subtle level of tension to the work.

1.20   The Fundamental Laws of Art

The above analyses of artworks have revealed powerful aspects of the structure of those works. This reinforces my claim that the artistic composition is the memory structure. That is, as I stated earlier:

The Fundamental Laws of Art = The Fundamental Laws of Memory Storage.

We have seen that the laws produce *process diagrams*, which give the actions *stored* in an artwork. That is, the diagrams actually represent the stored memory. Thus, according to this theory, the process of creating the work is that of loading histories into the work, and the process of understanding the work is the process of *recovering* those histories.

The painting analyses, carried out above, used three of my rules for recovering histories from curvature extrema. These rules are only three of the many rules to be elaborated in this book. All of them will reveal important aspects of the structure of artworks.

The three rules serve as a first illustration of a basic point to be argued in the book: All the rules of art come from the First and Second Fundamental Laws of Memory Storage. These are formulated respectively as the Asymmetry Principle and the Symmetry Principle. That is, the Asymmetry Principle and the Symmetry Principle are, in fact, the fundamental laws of art.

Let us now make sure we carefully understand this, as follows: The Asymmetry Principle states that any asymmetry in the present is assumed to have arisen from a past symmetry. And the Symmetry Principle states that any symmetry in the present is assumed to have always existed. Furthermore, to use these two laws, one goes through the simple three-part procedure given in section 1.4, for recovering the past. One merely partitions the present into its asymmetries and its symmetries. Then one applies the Asymmetry Principle to the asymmetries; and one applies the Symmetry Principle to the symmetries.

The three rules used in the above painting analyses were simply an example of this procedure. The first rule, the Symmetry-Curvature Duality Theorem, was an example of the partitioning of the shape into its asymmetries and symmetries. The rule said that there is one asymmetry (curvature extremum) for each symmetry (symmetry axis). The remaining two rules were each an example of the Symmetry Principle and Asymmetry Principle, respectively. That is, the particular example of the Symmetry Principle stated that the symmetry axes must be preserved over time, and this means that the processes must have gone along the symmetry axes. The particular example of the Asymmetry Principle stated that the different curvatures around the curve must become equal backwards in time.

The many sets of rules developed in this series of books will all have the three-part format just described. The only difference between the three rules just given, and the rules to be developed, is that the latter will be applied to different asymmetries and symmetries. That is, they will select different asymmetries and symmetries from the present, and apply the particular version of the Asymmetry Principle that corresponds to those particular asymmetries, and apply the particular version of the Symmetry Principle that corresponds to those particular symmetries.

The complete rule-system, for the analysis of artworks, is given by the entire set of asymmetries and symmetries that can be used in a work. Each type of asymmetry defines its own associated use of the Asymmetry Principle, and each type of symmetry defines its own associated use of the Symmetry Principle. The many rules of art are simply the many specific uses of the Asymmetry Principle and Symmetry Principle.

Chapter 2

Expressiveness of Line

2.1   Theory of Emotional Expression

A crucial phenomenon will now be introduced. When one looks over the diagrams produced for artworks on p28-40, something is immediately striking: The diagrams exhibit a considerable amount of the *emotional expression* of the works. This is a strange phenomenon. The diagrams were intended for one purpose only: to show the *process-history* recovered from the shapes. The arrows in the diagrams represent the actions that occurred in the recovered processes. Nevertheless, it is clear that, when one maps out the process-histories, one is mapping out the emotional content of the paintings. In fact, I will now propose the following basic law:

FUNDAMENTAL LAW OF EXPRESSION

Emotional expression is recovered process-history.

We shall see that this law is extremely valuable for analyzing paintings, for the following reason: Process-history is recovered by the rigorous and systematic set of recovery rules to be elaborated in the course of this book. Therefore, the powerful thing is that the rules will be able to rigorously and systematically map out the emotional content of artworks.

This goes completely against what people have believed. Since the beginning of art, it has always seemed impossible that the emotional content of an artwork can be rigorously and systematically determined. After all, we have been told, by countless books, that the emotions in an artwork are "ineffable", that they are so multiply and vaguely nuanced that one cannot explicitly define them.

43

This view existed because there was no theory of how emotional expression is captured in the structure of an artwork. Indeed there was no theory of artistic structure. What the present book does is to systematically elaborate the structure of artworks, and show the precise way in which the structure determines the emotional expression.

To fully understand how the book will accomplish this, it is necessary to show the progression from the first principles in Chapter 1 to the principles in this chapter. The progression is as follows. First begin with some of the basic principles of the previous chapter:

1. Shape is memory storage

2. Artworks are maximal memory stores.

3. Shape is the process-history recovered from the present state.

4. Tension goes from the present to the past state, i.e., corresponds to the recovery of process-history.

Using these principles, we can now turn to the emotional expression in an artwork. We shall see that the emotional expression corresponds to the recovered process-history. This is because the emotional expression is given by the configuration of tension. Thus, I propose the following:

EMOTIONAL EXPRESSION $\equiv$ MEMORY STORAGE

The emotional expression is given by the configuration of tension.

But tension is recovered process-history.

Therefore emotional expression is recovered process-history (i.e., memory storage).

Thus our rules for the recovery of process-history, i.e., memory storage, are the rules of emotional expression.

This allows us to systematically and completely map out the emotional expression in an artwork.

We can further understand this proposal by recognizing the fact that the word *emotion* consists of two components: *e* meaning *out*, and *motion* meaning *movement*. That is, emotion means *outward movement*. Therefore, the rules for recovering the process-histories, are the rules for recovering the outward movements (the e-motions) of the artist. Quite literally: The arrows that our rules draw on the paintings are the e-motions of the artist.

This chapter will demonstrate the above theory, with complete mathematical rigor, by working through an extremely important example: the expressiveness of line. Recall that the second half of the previous chapter studied the recovery of process-history from curvature. Curvature is the central concept in differential geometry. Therefore, by the above:

We will create the following systematic map:

Differential geometry $\longrightarrow$ **Emotional expression.**

2.2 Expressiveness of Line

Line is such a fundamental source of emotional expression in painting, that an individual who is not sensitive to line literally misses the painting.

Who can forget that first moment when one discovers line, perhaps in a Picasso or a Botticelli, and one's life changes forever; the whole world becoming a riot of line, every street-corner, every crowd, every face, every posture – one world-image of aliveness falling upon another as one dies into sleep at night. One fights to be lost from this lover, this demented fact about the world.

And with this truth tearing at one's life, one searches the books on art to find some understanding of line – this phenomenon to which all pay ultimate homage – and one finds hardly a single insight.

So one is thrown back upon one's own resources. But this turns out not to be a problem. For one discovers that to be sensitive to line is to know exactly how it works.

This book will map out a full and rigorous understanding of line, its expressive qualities, and how its structure achieves its expressive aims. This understanding will be systematic and complete in that it is elaborated from our fundamental laws and will follow from these laws in a comprehensive fashion.

2.3 The Four Types of Curvature Extrema

We are now going to develop a comprehensive theory of the *expressiveness of line*. This is done first by examining curvature extrema. The following fact will be crucial: There are actually four different types of curvature extrema. Furthermore, corresponding to these four types of extrema, there are four types of process-history. Since the above law says that there is a correspondence between emotional expression and recovered history, this means that there are four different types of emotional expression associated with curvature extrema.

Any curved line in a painting is a sequence of curvature extrema. Each of these comes from the vocabulary of four possible extrema. Thus, as one moves along the curve, one moves successively from one type of extremum to another. This means that

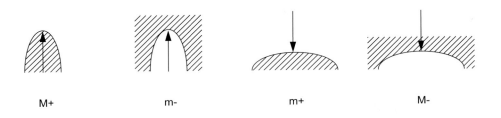

M+   m-   m+   M-

Figure 2.1: The four types of extrema.

the curve changes successively from one type of process-history to another. Now, since type of process-history corresponds to type of emotional expression, this means that the emotion changes successively along the curve. Thus, by identifying the successive extrema and their associated process-histories, we will be able to systematically map out the configuration of emotions expressed in a curve.

Let us now examine the four types of extrema. Each has its own particular shape as shown in Fig 2.1. It is important to carefully understand these four diagrams, as follows: First observe that each of the four diagrams shows a section of curve. On each section, the extremum is the central point.

Next observe that the curve is a boundary of some solid object, where the *solid* side of the boundary is indicated by the *shading*. Thus, the *non-shaded* side of the curve represents *empty space*.

Now observe that the curves in the first and second case are exactly the same shape. Despite this, there is a crucial difference between them: What is solid changes from one side of the curve to the other.

Similarly, the curves in the third and fourth case are the same shape as each other; but, again, the solid and empty space changes sides.

Artists refer to what has just been called "solid" as *positive space*. This is the *foreground*. Correspondingly "empty space" is generally called *negative space*. This is the *background*. What we can see from this is that the four types of extrema come in two pairs, where the distinction between the two members within a pair is a distinction between which side receives the positive space, and which side receives the negative space.

Every great artist completely integrates the shapes across positive and negative space. We shall see that this integration can exist only because the extrema occur in pairs like this. If this pairing were not a mathematical fact, then the major form of integration in any painting would not exist, and the impact of art would be considerably less.

Now, in my classification, each of the four extrema has its own label. The label consists of the letter M or m, together with the + or - sign.

The letters M and m mean respectively maximum and minimum; which will be explained later.

The + and - signs are immediately easy to understand: The + sign simply means that the solid side of the shape bends out. Correspondingly, the - sign means that the solid side of the shape bends in. Thus the first and third cases in Fig 2.1 are labeled "+" because the solid side of the curve bends out; and the second and fourth cases are labeled "-" because the solid side of the curve bends in.

What is crucial to remember is that the pair of symbols M and m are combined with the pair of symbols + and -, in all possible ways: which gives a total of four possible symbols: M^+, m^-, m^+, M^-. Now let us study these extrema carefully:

2.4 Process-Arrows for the Four Extrema

We first need to see why the process-arrows are assigned to the four extrema in the particular way shown in Fig 2.1.

Recall that the second of our three rules, for the inference of process-history from curvature extrema, says that the inferred process went along the symmetry axis leading to the extremum. Recall also that the symmetry axis is provided by the symmetry analysis I invented, called *Process Inferring Symmetry Analysis*, that is, *PISA* for short, described in section 1.9.

The symmetry axis created by PISA is defined with respect to the curve, and is not influenced by the side of the curve on which the positive and negative space are located. This means that the PISA symmetry axis is in the same position with respect to the first two extrema, because these two curves have the same shape as each other. Furthermore, the PISA symmetry axis is in the same position with respect to the other two extrema, because these two curves also have the same shape as each other.

From Fig 2.1 the reader can see where these axes are, because, by our inference rules, the process-arrows are put exactly along the axes.

A crucial fact should now be recognized, which we will later see is fundamentally important to art and the rigorous analysis of artistic expression: As can be seen from Fig 2.1, the PISA symmetry axis is on the *convex* side of the curve for the first two extrema, but on the *concave* side of the curve for the other two extrema.

Placing the symmetry axes on the concave side for the latter two extrema seems very strange. One would expect the axis to be "between" the two sides of the curve. This would mean that the axis would be on the convex side, i.e., below the curve rather than above it as shown. Indeed, in the first two extrema, this is exactly where the axis is. What accounts for the strange position of the axis for the other two extrema?

In fact, the answer comes from my proof of the Symmetry-Curvature Duality Theorem, in Leyton [12]. I proved that PISA symmetry axes, for the four extrema, are positioned exactly as shown in Fig 2.1.

No other symmetry axis in the history of mathematics has this property. That is, all other axes would be "between" the sides of the curve; i.e., on the convex side; i.e., below the curves, in all four cases in Fig 2.1. For example, the axes of Blum [1] and Brady [2] would have these conventional positions.

The fact that the PISA symmetry axis has the unconventional positions shown is profoundly important for the analysis of artworks, as we shall see. In the remainder of this section, I will give a brief glimpse into the reason, but will discuss it in considerable detail later in the chapter.

By our inference rules, the symmetry axis gives the inferred process. Notice that, in the first two extrema, the inferred process is responsible for the *sharpening* at the extremum, relative to the flattening at each end of the same curve. Thus the process-arrow is exactly where we would expect it, in order to create the sharpening; i.e., the arrow is below the curve and pushing upward. This means that the symmetry axis is in the correct position for these two extrema.

Now, in the other two extrema, observe that the inferred process is responsible for the *flattening* at the extremum, relative to the sharpening at each end of the same curve. Thus the process-arrow is exactly where we would expect it, in order to create the flattening; i.e., the arrow is above the curve and pushing downward. This means that the symmetry axis is in the correct position for these two extrema.

Thus, PISA gives the symmetry axes exactly where one would expect the processes. This is why I called it *Process-Inferring Symmetry Analysis*. The profound importance of this, for rigorously capturing the emotional expression of paintings, will now be seen.

2.5   Historical Characteristics of Extrema

In this section, I will argue that, from each of the four curvature extrema, one recovers a different process-history. Since, according to section 2.1, the recovered process-history is the emotional expression, this means that each curvature extremum has a different emotional expression.

I will show that the process-history recovered from an extremum has six characteristics. They will be called the *historical characteristics* of the extremum.

Now, since the recovered process-history is the emotional expression, the historical characteristics are the characteristics of the emotional expression of the extremum.

> **There are six characteristics of the process-history at an extremum, and therefore there are six characteristics of the emotion expressed by an extremum.**

These six characteristics are crucial to the expressiveness of line. Each curvature extremum, on a line, possesses its six characteristics. A great artist is fully aware of them and exploits them.

> **One can literally take a walk around a canvas and see that, at each extremum, the artist has been completely aware of the six expressive characteristics of the extremum, and has fully exploited all six.**

Not a single characteristic can be ignored because it is there, whether the artist likes it or not; and a bad artist is one who is not sensitive to its presence, or cannot use it.

And for the viewer, it is impossible to "read" what is going on in a work of art if one is not sensitive to the following six characteristics. The characteristics are:

(1) Penetrative vs. Compressive

I will say that the first characteristic of the history recovered from an extremum is that is either *penetrative* or *compressive*. Consider Fig 2.1 (p46) again. *The first two extrema will be called penetrative and the last two will be called compressive.* It is necessary to carefully understand why I have chosen these descriptions, as follows:

Return to the Picasso *Still-Life*, shown in Plate 1. In section 1.19.1 (p27), a map was produced of processes derived from the curvature extrema via the three rules for the recovery of history from extrema (recall Fig 1.18, page 28). It is important now to understand that this map showed only some of the processes recovered by the three rules. Many of the processes were omitted simply to avoid over-crowding the map. However, the three rules should have been applied to every single extremum in the painting, to recover the associated processes. Each extremum contributes a process via the three rules, and each is visually a part of the composition of the painting.

What we are now going to do is to look at some of the processes previously omitted. The first concern will be the yellow jug, in the top left of the painting (Plate 1). This jug has considerable expressive beauty. And yet it will been shown that this expressiveness can be completely and systematically understood. The expressiveness is its recovered history, and this history can be entirely mapped out via our rules for the recovery of history.

At this point, only one part of the jug will be considered: The line that swings backwards and forwards down its right side. This line has four extrema. They are shown with their associated process-arrows in Fig 2.2. The object, into which, and out of which, the line swings, is the jug. Let us look carefully at what this implies:

The jug is a solid object, the foreground – i.e., what artists call positive space. The space to the right of it is the background – i.e., negative space. Any great artist makes the positive space and negative space contribute equally to the structure of a painting. This is an essential aspect of unification.

Now, as one moves down the line, one finds, that, at the top extremum, the positive space pushes into the negative space; then, at the next extremum, the negative space pushes back into the positive space; and so on. This means that the positive space and negative space alternately push into each other, i.e., *intrude* into each other. We will therefore say that each of these four processes is *penetrative*.

It is important to understand which types of extrema are involved. Since the top extremum involves the positive space pushing into the negative space, this extremum must, according to Fig 2.1 (p46), be the M^+ extremum. This is because the shading in Fig 2.1 represents the positive space, and the shaded side of M^+ pushes *into* the non-shaded side.

The next extremum, down the side of the jug, involves the negative space pushing into the positive space. According to Fig 2.1, this extremum must be m^-, because the non-shaded side in Fig 2.1 represents the negative space, and the non-shaded side of m^- pushes *into* the shaded side.

By this argument, the third and fourth extrema, down the side of the jug, must be M^+ and m^- respectively.

Therefore, what has been illustrated here is that, of the four types of extrema that can

Figure 2.2: Oscillating extrema on the jug.

exist, the M^+ and the m^- are the penetrative extrema. That is, their recovered arrows penetrate the space towards which they point.

Let us now turn from the penetrative extrema to the other type of extrema, which I call the *compressive* extrema. To see examples of the latter, return again to the Picasso, and this time look at the dish of fruit at the top right of the painting (Plate 1). Again, this structure has considerable expressive force, and again we will see that this expressiveness can be completely and systematically understood.

A significant portion of the expressive force of the dish of fruit comes from the use of compressive extrema. Picasso employs a number of them in this situation. In order to see them, first observe that the dish of fruit involves three overlapping ellipses, as shown in the three parts of Fig 2.3. The ellipses are respectively, (a) the central apple, (b) the right part of the dish, and (c) the left part of the dish.

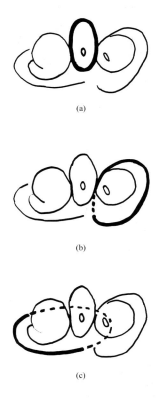

(a)

(b)

(c)

Figure 2.3: Three ellipses in the fruit dish

We shall see that an ellipse has *two penetrative and two compressive extrema*, and Picasso exploits this fact, in building up the expressive power of the dish of fruit. A penetrative extremum has a very different emotional quality from a compressive extremum, and this is due to the very different histories involved. In order to understand these differences, let us now take an ellipse and study it carefully.

Fig 2.4 shows an ellipse. Any ellipse has a total of four extrema. These have been marked on the diagram. The two points, at the left and right ends of the ellipse, are extrema at which curvature (bend) is *maximal*; i.e., a car driving around this curve would have the steering wheel turned *most* at these two points. Conversely, the top and bottom points are *minima* of curvature; i.e., a car driving around this curve would have the steering wheel turned *least* at these two points – i.e., the steering wheel would point almost straight ahead. These two points of least curvature are also called extrema, because to be the *least* is also to be *extreme*.

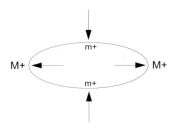

Figure 2.4: An ellipse has four extrema, and therefore four processes.

On this diagram, the arrows have also been placed indicating the histories inferred from these four extrema. Rigorously, they are the symmetry axes defined by my PISA definition of symmetry, as discussed in section 2.4.

In order to understand these recovered histories, one must first recall that, according to the Asymmetry Principle, the past of any smooth closed shape is a circle. Thus the past of this ellipse must have been a circle.

One can imagine, for example, that the object with which we are dealing is an ordinary plastic beach-ball, which is spherical when no force is pushing on it. In order to push it into the shape of an ellipse, we have compressed it vertically between our hands. The top and bottom arrows show the compressive action. This has forced the top and bottom points of the circle to go inwards, as shown by the vertical arrows, creating the two m^+ extrema. To compensate, the air pressure, inside the ball, has forced the left and right end-points to move outwards, as shown by the two horizontal arrows in the diagram. These latter two arrows created the two M^+ extrema, at either end. M^+ extrema are always penetrative. In this example, they represent the fact that the ball (positive space) has pushed out into the surrounding air (negative space).

However, the m^+ extrema, on the top and bottom of the ellipse, are very different. Here, the negative space pushes towards the positive space of the ball, but has not penetrated it. I call this action *compressive*.

> *The ellipse illustrates very clearly the difference between penetrative and compressive extrema. In both cases, a force from one space (positive or negative) acts on the other. However, in the penetrative case, the force actually invades the latter space, whereas in the compressive case, it does not.*

This effect is exploited very strongly in the dish of fruit, in the Picasso. Fig 2.5a shows the compressive forces acting on those m^+ extrema that are visible. Thus the two horizontal forces on the central apple squash it between the two fruit on either side. These two forces are inferred from the two m^+ extrema, that constitute the two sides of the central fruit. Again, from the m^+ extremum on the right side of the dish, one infers another compressive force, acting on the dish from the right. Finally, from the m^+ extremum at the bottom of the dish, one infers a strong upward force that exerts a considerable pressure at that extremum.

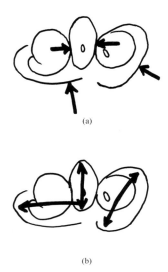

(a)

(b)

Figure 2.5: (a) Compressive forces. (b) Penetrative forces.

These compressive forces contrast very strongly with the penetrative forces, which are shown in Fig 2.5b. They are inferred from the M^+ extrema. Observe how each one is experienced as invading the surrounding space.

One can go around each of the extrema in the entire painting, and see how each is either penetrative or compressive – and see also how Picasso exploits these two historical alternatives as strong expressive effects.

We are now going to see that penetrative and compressive extrema differ not only with respect to the invasive vs. non-invasive distinction in their histories, but also with respect to other historical properties. Picasso exploits each of these properties, as does any great artist.

Before going on to the next historical characteristic, let us introduce a term that will be useful: *recipient space*. The recipient space is the space that receives the action defined by the process-arrow. In any situation, it is easy to identify this space, as follows:

RECIPIENT SPACE

A process-arrow lies on one side of the curve. The space on the other side of the curve will be called the recipient space. That is, the recipient space is the space to which the process-arrow points.

To illustrate, let us return to the beach-ball in Fig 2.4. Consider first the two end M^+ process-arrows. They lie on one side of the curve. The space on the other side is the air surrounding the ball. This is the space to which the arrows point. The recipient space of the M^+ arrows is therefore the air surrounding the ball.

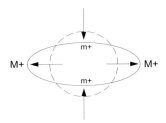

Figure 2.6: An ellipse with the circle from which it was produced.

In contrast, let us now consider the two vertical m^+ arrows. The ball is on the other side of the curve from these two arrows. The two arrows therefore point towards the ball. Thus the ball is the recipient space of the two m^+ arrows.

(2) Sharpening vs. Flattening

The second characteristic of the recovered history can be understood by looking again at the ellipse. An ellipse will be used a number of times in the explanation of the historical characteristics, because it is the simplest shape which contains both a penetrative and a compressive extremum. For ease of exposition, we will continue to regard the ellipse as a spherical beach-ball that has been compressed, e.g., between two hands.

In Fig 2.6, the superimposed dashed line shows the initial circular shape of the beach-ball; and the solid line shows the ellipse into which the ball has been compressed. Let us consider what happened in the process-history at the curvature extrema.

First consider either one of the two penetrative extrema (M^+) at the two ends of the ellipse. When comparing the curvature at the M^+ extremum with the corresponding point on the circle from which it came, one can see that the M^+ extremum has greater curvature (bend) than the corresponding point on the circle. Thus the history that changed the point on the circle into the extremum M^+ on the ellipse was a process of *sharpening* the curvature.

In contrast, consider either one of the two compressive extrema (m^+) at the top and bottom of the ellipse. When comparing the curvature at the m^+ extremum with the corresponding point on the circle from which it came, one sees that the m^+ extremum has less curvature (bend) than the corresponding point on the circle. Thus the history that changed the point on the circle into the extremum m^+ on the ellipse was a process of *flattening* the curvature.

In consequence: a crucial difference between the history inferred from a penetrative extremum and the history inferred from a compressive extremum is that the former creates a sharpening of curvature, and the latter creates a flattening of curvature.

Observe that these are characteristics of the *inferred* histories. That is, the past state, the circle, is not actually visible. It is inferred via the Asymmetry Principle.

This inference has lead to the conclusion that the sharpest point, on the shape in the present, was previously flatter; and that the flattest point, on the shape in the present, was previously sharper.

This is a crucial expressive aspect of lines in art. Thus, for example, let us return to the Picasso *Still-Life*. Consider the top and bottom extrema of the middle apple on the fruit dish, in Fig 2.5b. These are M^+ extrema. The history inferred from them is that they were previously flatter. Similarly, consider the side extrema of this apple, in Fig 2.5a. These are m^+ extrema. The history inferred from them is that they were previously sharper.

(3) Tightening vs. Broadening (Closing vs. Opening)

The previous historical characteristic, sharpening vs. flattening, is an effect that will be regarded as acting at the extremum point itself. This is because the effect is strongest at that point.

In contrast to this sharpening vs. flattening effect, the historical characteristic we now examine, tightening vs. broadening, concerns the effect on the curve surrounding the extremum. This effect also possesses an expressiveness that is exploited by the artist. Let us try to understand what it is:

Let us return again to the example of the ellipse. Fig 2.7a and 2.7b show, respectively, a penetrative extremum and a compressive extremum taken from the ellipse. The penetrative extremum (left) has been oriented vertically to make comparison easier with the compressive extremum (right). In both cases, the dashed line indicates the starting circle.

(a)   (b)

Figure 2.7: Tightening vs. broadening effect.

Now observe the following: The arrows in Fig 2.7a show what happened to the circle in producing the penetrative extremum: The two sides of the circle were pushed towards each other, to become the two sides of the extremum. This effect can be described as *tightening* or *closing* the curve. In contrast, the arrows in Fig 2.7b show what happened to the circle in producing the compressive extremum: The two sides of the circle were pulled apart from each other, to become the two sides of the extremum. This effect can be described as *broadening* or *opening* the curve.

To emphasize: When comparing the directions of the arrows in Fig 2.7a and 2.7b, one sees that they are in opposite directions – the arrows in Fig 2.7a push inwards, and the arrows in Fig 2.7b pull outwards.

This contrasting effect, tightening vs. broadening, is exploited enormously by artists, as will be seen. For example, in great portraits, faces are essentially structures of curvature extrema. We shall see that the artist carefully chooses between the tightening and broadening extrema to convey the character of the person being portrayed.

(4) Facilitative vs. Oppositional

This characteristic of the recovered history can again be illustrated with the simplest example, the ellipse, understood as a squashed beach-ball.

Return to Fig 2.4 (p52) which shows the arrangement of process-arrows around the ellipse. What should be observed now is the following: For the penetrative extrema, the arrows occur on the inside; whereas for the compressive extrema, the arrows occur on the outside. This fact becomes crucial for the emotional expressiveness of line, as will be seen soon in the analyses of paintings. The basis of this phenomenon should be carefully understood, as follows:

At first, the reader might think that the penetrative arrows have been placed on the inside, and the compressive arrows on the outside, because this arrangement describes the physical situation being used as an illustration: the squashed beach-ball. However, this is definitely not the reason. The real reason will now be given, and it is crucial for the reader to understand it.

A shape has been given in the present, an ellipse. There is no extra information. For example, there are no arrows – since they represent the process-history. The goal is to *recover* the process-history. In fact, it will be recovered from the shape. Chapter 1 showed that, in order to recover the process-history from a shape's curvature extrema, it is necessary to apply three rules, which must be carefully examined again:

> (1) The Symmetry-Curvature Duality Theorem: This says that each curvature extremum has a unique axis leading to, and terminating at, the extremum.

> (2) The Symmetry Principle applied to symmetry axes (Interaction Principle): The processes, which created the shape, went along symmetry axes.

> (3) The Asymmetry Principle applied to curvature variation: Differences in curvature must be removed backwards in time.

When one looks at these three rules, one discovers that they introduce three objects in succession, each depending on the previous object:

curvature extrema $\longrightarrow$ symmetry axes $\longrightarrow$ processes

That is, one finds the curvature extrema in order to find the symmetry axes, and one finds the symmetry axes in order to find the processes. In particular, one finds the symmetry axes before finding the processes, because it is the symmetry axes that tell one where the processes lie: i.e., the processes are conjectured as lying along the symmetry axes.

This means that the arrows (i.e., histories), shown on the ellipse, are really placed where the symmetry axes are.

A mathematical result, that I proved in Leyton [12] shows that, for an ellipse, two of the symmetry axes occur on the outside and two occur on the inside. In fact, this is the result discussed in section 2.4. That is, it is part of the proof of the Symmetry-Curvature Duality Theorem, and shows that in the four curvature extrema, M^+, m^-, m^+, M^-, the symmetry axes for the first two extrema lie on the convex side of the curve and the symmetry axes of the last two extrema lie on the concave side.

We are now ready to understand the *emotional* consequences of this. By the Fundamental Law of Expression (section 2.1), the emotional expression is given by the recovered history. So we need to consider the histories that are aligned along the symmetry axes; i.e., the histories shown in Fig 2.4 (p52). The expressive characteristic to be observed now is the relationship between the recovered history and the curve itself, as follows:

Any extremum can be regarded as an arch, which points in a certain direction. Thus, Fig 2.8 shows a penetrative and a compressive extremum. Notice that each can be considered to be an arch. Most crucially, the dashed arrow on each shows the *direction of arching*. (Later, it will be shown how to rigorously construct the dashed arrow.)

(a)   (b)

Figure 2.8: Direction of arching on a penetrative and compressive extremum.

Now let us consider the penetrative extremum on the left of the ellipse in Fig 2.4 (p52). It is clear that the direction of arching is towards the left of the page. Thus, if we drew in the dashed arrow, indicating the direction of arching, it would coincide with the arrow already drawn there, which represents the recovered history. We shall say therefore that the latter arrow (the recovered history) *facilitates* the direction of arching.

Let us now contrast this with a compressive extremum at the top of the ellipse. The direction of arching at this extremum is upwards – as can be seen in Fig 2.8b. This means that the arrow shown as coming *downwards* from above the ellipse on p52, i.e., the arrow indicating the recovered history, actually opposes the direction of arching. We will say that the history is *oppositional* to the direction of arching.

Thus, to summarize:

A penetrative history is facilitative to the direction of arching.

A compressive history is oppositional to the direction of arching.

This property, facilitative vs. oppositional, is a characteristic of the recovered history, as follows: The direction in which the curve arches, exists before one infers the history. It is a property of the curve as it occurs, in front of one, in the present. It is only after one applies the three rules for the recovery of history that one can see whether the recovered history facilitates the direction of arching, or opposes it.

This historical characteristic, facilitative vs. oppositional, is a crucial expressive factor exploited by all great artists. For example, the artist will insert oppositional extrema into the outline of a person's head to indicate literally, that the person has an oppositional personality. This will soon be illustrated with paintings by Holbein, Gauguin, and Hans Memling.

Important Example: The Bay

For each of the historical characteristics discussed so far, a single example was used as an illustration: the ellipse (as positive space). However, even though the ellipse has four extrema, they are examples of M^+ and m^+, which are only two of the four types of extrema. Restricting ourselves to this example has given us some familiarity with these two types. However, most paintings contain all four types, and great paintings exploit all four with tremendous expressive effect. Thus, it is necessary to become familiar with the remaining two types.

Fig 2.9 shows, again, all four types. The two examined so far are the first and third. It is now necessary to familiarize ourselves with the second and fourth. Fortunately, there is another shape, almost as simple as an ellipse, which can be used to easily gain an

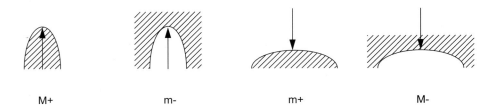

M+   m-   m+   M-

Figure 2.9: The four types of extrema.

understanding of the remaining two extrema. This example turns out to be enormously important to understand. For when we understand it, we will finally be liberated to understand the structure of any line in a painting, no matter how complicated.

The example is that of a *bay*, in a coast-line. For instance, Fig 2.10 shows an island in the ocean, and, in the upper half of the island, there is a bay.

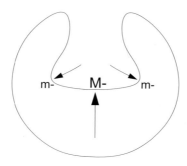

Figure 2.10: A bay in an island.

Let us consider the standard way in which a bay is formed. It can be illustrated with this island: Initially, the island was *circular*. At some point in time, there was an inflow of water at the top part of the coast-line. Therefore, that part started to dip inwards. However, as the water continued to go further into the island, it eventually encountered a ridge of mountains, along the central horizontal line of the island. This ridge of mountains acted as a resistance against the water flowing further in this direction. Thus the water started to bulge out to either side, and the bay began to form. This lead to the shape shown in Fig 2.10.

By examining this figure carefully, we can see exactly all the factors involved. Consider first the central point of the bay. It is labeled M^-. This is a curvature extremum. It marks the flattest part of the bay.

Now, this flattening was caused by the resistance of the mountains in the island. Observe that, below the M^-, there is an upward arrow leading to the M^-. This indicates the resisting effect of the mountains. The arrow corresponds to the symmetry axis created by my PISA definition of symmetry.

Let us now move sideways along the bay to either end. The next extremum we encounter is m^-. There is one m^- at each end of the bay. Each has its own arrow pointing into the island, i.e., on the side of the water. These two m^- arrows represent the water moving inwards, but also being forced sideways because of the resistance of the mountains in the island.

We can therefore see that the bay contains the two remaining types of extrema: m^- and M^-. What is necessary now is to examine these two types in terms of the historical characteristics considered so far, thus:

(1) Penetrative vs. Compressive.

Fig 2.11 shows the positive space (island) as shaded and the negative space (water) as non-shaded. This allows us to consider the characteristic of penetrative vs. compressive. First consider the two m^- extrema, one at each end of the bay. Since they represent the water moving inward, they are *penetrative*. It is necessary to carefully understand this, as follows:

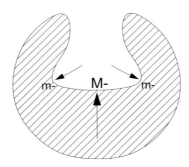

Figure 2.11: Positive and negative space on a bay.

Consider again Fig 2.9 p58, which shows the four types of extrema. I called the first two *penetrative* because, in both cases, the space in which the arrow is located invades the opposite space. That is, in the case of M^+, the positive space (shaded) invades the negative space (non-shaded); and in the case of m^-, the negative space (non-shaded) invades the positive space (shaded). Notice that, in the other two extrema, m^+ and M^-, this invasive effect does not exist.

Thus we see that, at the m^- extrema in bay of the island, (Fig 2.11), the negative space (water) invades the positive space (land).

Let us now turn to the M^- extremum in the center of the bay. Notice that its arrow is located within the island, the positive space. Furthermore, it is directed towards the water, the negative space. Thus, it represents the action of the positive space on the negative space. However, the positive space does not penetrate the negative space. It merely compresses the negative space. Thus one sees here, an example of our general rule that the history inferred from any M^- extremum is *compressive*.

Observe also that the structure of the bay in Fig 2.11 is exactly the structure given for the M^- extremum in Fig 2.9 p58 – the diagram has been merely turned around.

To summarize: We are using the bay to illustrate the historical characteristics of the m^- and M^- extrema. We have just finished examining these two extrema in relation to the first historical characteristic, penetrative vs. compressive. The example illustrates that the history inferred from m^- is penetrative, whereas the history inferred from M^- is compressive.

(2) Sharpening vs. Flattening

Given what has been said so far about the bay, the remaining historical characteristics of m^- and M^- are easy to understand, as will now be seen.

The second characteristic of the history inferred from an extremum concerns the effect at the extremum point itself. It concerns whether the inferred history is understood as having caused a sharpening or a flattening at that point. Consider either of the m^- processes in Fig 2.11. Clearly, it has induced a sharpening at the extremum. In contrast, the M^- process at the center of the bay has induced a flattening at the extremum.

(3) Tightening vs. Broadening (Closing vs. Opening)

Whereas the previous historical characteristic concerns the effect of the inferred process at the extremum point itself, this third characteristic concerns the effect of the inferred process on the surrounding curve.

Once again, by looking at either of the m^- processes in Fig 2.11, one can see that the effect of this process is to pull together the curve on either side of the extremum – an effect I called tightening or closing.

In contrast, by looking at the M^- process in Fig 2.11, one sees that the effect of this process is to push apart the curve on either side of the extremum – an effect I called broadening or opening.

(4) Facilitative vs. Oppositional

Recall that any extremum can be described as an arch that points in a certain direction. For example, recall that Fig 2.8 (p57) shows a penetrative and compressive extremum, each with a dashed arrow indicating the direction of arching. The historical characteristic, facilitative vs. oppositional, concerns whether the inferred history is co-incident with the direction of arching, i.e., facilitates the arching, or whether the inferred history pushes against the direction of arching, i.e., opposes the arching.

Now let us consider one of the m^- extrema in Fig 2.11. It is an arch. The direction of the arch is diagonally downwards. Thus, if we drew in the dashed arrow, indicating this direction, it would coincide with the arrow already drawn there, which represents the recovered history. One can see therefore that the latter arrow, the recovered history, facilitates the direction of arching.

Let us now contrast this with the M^- extremum at the center of the bay in Fig 2.11. This part of the bay is clearly an arch. As an arch, it happens to point downwards. Thus the dashed arrow, indicating the direction of arching, would oppose the upward arrow shown, which represents the compressive effect. This illustrates the fact that the process-history inferred from any M^- extremum is oppositional.

Comment

We have now gained some familiarity with all four extrema. Two were discussed in the simple example of the ellipse, and two were discussed in the simple example of the bay. Return to Fig 2.9 p58, which shows the four kinds of extrema. The first and third occur in the ellipse, and the second and fourth occur in the bay.

Each extremum has six historical characteristics, of which four have now been discussed. It remains therefore to describe the final two historical characteristics.

(5) Outward vs. Inward

This fifth historical characteristic concerns the relation of the inferred process to the positive space (solid object). Is the process *outward* or *inward*, relative to that space?

Fig 2.12 shows the two shape examples that we have used as illustrations: the ellipse and the bay. As usual, the shaded area represents the positive space, and the non-shaded area represents the negative space. Notice that all four extrema are represented here: M^+ and m^+ occur in the ellipse, and m^- and M^- occur in the bay.

Figure 2.12: Positive space on ellipse and bay.

The diagrams in Fig 2.12 illustrate which extrema generally have an outward process and which extrema have an inward process, thus:

$$M^+ \longleftrightarrow \text{outward}$$
$$m^- \longleftrightarrow \text{inward}$$
$$m^+ \longleftrightarrow \text{inward}$$
$$M^- \longleftrightarrow \text{outward.}$$

(6) Process-Type

All the historical characteristics given so far have divided the extrema into pairs. To understand this, consider again Fig 2.9 p58, showing the four extrema in one row. The first historical characteristic, penetrative vs. compressive, classified the first two extrema as penetrative and the last two as compressive. In contrast, the fifth historical characteristic, outward vs. inward, classified the first and last extrema as outward, and the second and third extrema as inward. Thus, although each historical characteristic classifies the extrema into two pairs, the pairings were not always the same.

The final historical characteristic has the purpose of breaking all pairs, thus recognizing each extremum in its own right as different.

This characteristic will simply be called *process-type*. It exploits the fact that each of the four extrema corresponds to a different process word in English, as will now be seen. By looking at the row of four extrema, Fig 2.9 p58, these four words are as follows:

M^+, the first extremum, always corresponds to the word *protrusion*. This is clear because it shows the solid as protruding into the empty space.

m^-, the second extremum, always corresponds to the word *indentation*. This is clear because it shows a force going into the solid, from the outside, i.e., indenting.

m^+, the third extremum, always corresponds to the word *squashing*. This is clear because it shows the force as squashing the positive space. Recall, for example, that this extremum corresponded to the hands at the top and bottom of the beach ball, squashing the ball.

M^-, the final extremum, always corresponds to the word *resistance*. It is a force, from the object, resisting something coming from the outside. For example, in the previous figure, this extremum occurred in the center of the bay, where its process represented the mountains, within the island, resisting the inward flow of water.

$$M^+ \longleftrightarrow \text{protrusion}$$
$$m^- \longleftrightarrow \text{indentation}$$
$$m^+ \longleftrightarrow \text{squashing}$$
$$M^- \longleftrightarrow \text{resistance.}$$

2.6 The Role of the Historical Characteristics

Let us try to understand what we have been doing: A painting is a static frozen object in the present. Nothing in it actually moves. However, I have proposed that the laws of artistic composition are the laws for recovering history from the present. Using these laws, every aspect of the work is converted into memory, i.e., information about the past. In fact, I argue that the artwork gains its aesthetic effect by becoming a memory-object.

We have been examining the rules for recovering history from *curvature extrema*. We have seen that there are three such rules. For each curvature extremum, the rules

Table 2.1: **CHARACTERISTICS OF INFERRED HISTORY**

(1) Action on recipient space
(2) Action on extremum point
(3) Action on surrounding curve
(4) Action in relation to arching
(5) Action in relation to positive space
(6) Process-type

	(1)	**(2)**	**(3)**	**(4)**	**(5)**	**(6)**
M^+	penetrative	sharpening	tightening	facilitative	outward	protrusion
m^-	penetrative	sharpening	tightening	facilitative	inward	indentation
m^+	compressive	flattening	broadening	oppositional	inward	squashing
M^-	compressive	flattening	broadening	oppositional	outward	resistance

infer the historical process as having pushed the curve along its associated symmetry axis and created the extremum. Every extremum provides this historical structure.

However, while all extrema share this historical structure, the process in each case achieves this structure in different ways. That is, for each extremum, the historical process has a particular way in which it has pushed the curve along the axis to create the extremum. For example, the inferred process acted either by sharpening or flattening, and either by going inward or outward; and so on. I have called these, the historical characteristics.

It is time now to gather the six historical characteristics of each extremum into one table – Table 2.1. We will soon be returning to the analysis of paintings, and when we do, this table will be crucial to understanding how the artist achieved the complex emotion expressed in the work.

Table 2.1 is organized as follows: The top half of the table lists the six historical characteristics. Each one is now given a title, e.g., the first one is called action on recipient space. The bottom half of the table lists the four extrema. The row for an extremum is the set of six individual values that the extremum takes with respect to the six characteristics listed above.

Minor comment: In any row all characteristics are given by adjectives, except the last, which is given by a noun. Although this is awkward in the table, it will nevertheless be convenient in the discussions.

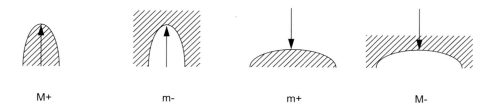

M+   m-   m+   M-

Figure 2.13: The four types of extrema.

2.7   The Duality Operator

A new rule will now be proposed that gives enormous insight into the structure of artworks. It will be called the *Duality Operator, D.*

The Duality Operator, D, reverses foreground and background, i.e., it exchanges positive and negative space.

What will reveal so much about the structure of the artwork is an examination of how this operator acts on the histories inferred from the curvature extrema. That is, we have three basic rules for the inference of process-history from curvature extrema. It is necessary to examine what the Duality Operator does to these inferred histories.

Let us begin by examining the effect of the operator on the curvature extrema themselves. Fig 2.13 again shows the four extrema. Now we have noted many times that the first and second extremum have exactly the same curve; their only difference is that the positive and negative spaces have switched sides. However, this exchange of sides is exactly what the Duality Operator achieves. Therefore, one can say, quite simply, that the Duality Operator transforms extremum M^+ into extremum m^-, and vice versa. This effect is described as follows:

$$M^+ \longleftrightarrow m^-$$

the double arrow indicating that the Duality Operator goes in *both* directions between the first and second extremum.

Also, we have observed that the third and fourth extremum have exactly the same curve; their only difference being that the positive and negative spaces have switched sides. Therefore, again, one can say that the Duality Operator transforms extremum m^+ into extremum M^-, and vice versa. This effect is described as follows:

$$m^+ \longleftrightarrow M^-$$

This means that one can define the action of the Duality Operator on curvature extrema, in the following way:

Duality Operator, D.

$$M^+ \longleftrightarrow m^- \qquad m^+ \longleftrightarrow M^-$$

M^+ and m^- will be called each others *duals*. Similarly, m^+ and M^- will be called each others *duals*.

We now come on to what will turn out to be a fundamental issue in the structure of artworks: the effect of the Duality Operator on the *histories* inferred from curvature extrema. The reason why this issue is fundamental is that, according to our argument, the structure of the artwork is the process-history inferred from the work. The history gives the tension structure of the work. The history also equals the emotion expressed by the work. It will now be argued that the Duality Operator is basic to unifying the tension in an artwork, and unifying the emotion expressed by the work. That is, the operator is basic to turning the work into an integrated whole – structurally and emotionally.

Thus, let us proceed to examine the effect of the Duality Operator on the histories inferred from the curvature extrema. Fig 2.13 p65 shows the row of four extrema, together with the process-arrows inferred from the extrema via our three basic rules. The arrows are the *traces*, the *histories*, of the curvature extrema as they were formed, i.e., as the curve was pushed along the axes.

What is necessary to recognize is the following fundamental fact:

The process-arrows are unchanged under the action of the Duality Operator.

Let us understand this carefully using Fig 2.13 p65. The Duality Operator goes between the first and the second extremum, M^+ and m^-, switching the sides of the positive and negative space. However, despite this, the operator does not switch the sides of the process-arrow. As can be seen from the diagram, the process-arrow remains exactly in the same place. This is because the arrow is the symmetry axis of the *curve*, which is the same in the two cases, independent of positive and negative space.

Similarly, the Duality Operator goes between the third and the fourth extremum, m^+ and M^-, switching the sides of the positive and negative space. However, despite this, the operator does not switch the sides of the process-arrow. Again, as can be seen from Fig 2.13 p65, the process-arrow remains exactly in the same place, because the *curve* is the same.

I argue that the fact that the Duality Operator leaves the process-arrow unchanged, is fundamental to art: As we shall see, it is crucial to the integration (unity) of the artwork.

It is necessary now to go more deeply into the relation between the Duality Operator and the history inferred from curvature extrema. We need to examine the relationship between the Duality Operator and the *six historical characteristics*. It will be seen that this relationship is fundamental to understanding any artwork.

The six historical characteristics define six components or aspects of the process-history inferred from a curvature extremum. It is necessary to establish which characteristics remain unchanged under the Duality Operator, as it transforms an extremum into its dual. The answer is the following: The first four historical characteristics are unchanged under the Duality Operator. This is easy to check, as follows:

Consider M^+ and its dual m^-. Table 2.1 gives the six historical characteristics for M^+ and m^- as:

	(1)	(2)	(3)	(4)	(5)	(6)
M^+	penetrative	sharpening	tightening	facilitative	outward	protrusion
m^-	penetrative	sharpening	tightening	facilitative	inward	indentation

By looking at these two rows, we see that the first four characteristics for M^+ are the same as the first four characteristics for m^-. However, we can also see from these rows that the fifth and sixth characteristics for M^+ are not the same as the fifth and sixth characteristics for m^-.

Exactly the same phenomenon occurs with extremum m^+ and its dual M^-, as can easily be checked by looking at Table 2.1 p64.

Generally, therefore, we conclude the following:

> **In transforming any extremum into its dual, the Duality Operator preserves the first four characteristics and alters the last two.**

This statement is crucial for the following reasons. The Fundamental Law of Expression says that emotional expression is recovered history. This means that the six historical characteristics are six characteristics of the emotion expressed by the extrema.

> **The above statement tells us precisely which emotional characteristics are transferred in going from positive to negative space and which are altered.**

This remarkable fact will soon be illustrated by studying one of Picasso's paintings from the Blue period. First, however, it is necessary to emphasize a crucial issue that is involved in what has just been said – the issue of integration:

Let us gather together the set of historical properties that are preserved under the Duality Operator. It was shown earlier that the process-arrow is unchanged by the action of the Duality Operator. Furthermore, it was shown that the first four historical characteristics are also preserved by the action of the Duality Operator. This gives us a total of five historical properties that are preserved by the operator. Their role is crucial for the following reason:

> **The fact that the Duality Operator preserves the process-arrow and the first four historical characteristics, is fundamental in allowing unification across positive and negative space.**

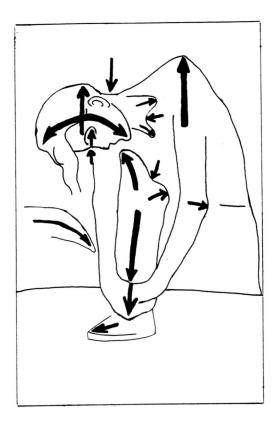

Figure 2.14: Processes leading to extrema in Picasso's *Woman Ironing*.

2.8 Picasso: *Woman Ironing*

In order to consider the issues involved in the unification of foreground and background, let us examine Picasso's *Woman Ironing*, given in the color Plate 5.

Fig 2.14 shows some of the main curvature extrema with their inferred processes. Like any great artist, Picasso integrates positive and negative space. In this painting, he achieves this integration in the following way: He makes the shape of the woman's body, the same as the shape that she encloses, as follows:

Consider Fig 2.15. The outer solid line is the outline of her body – going along the outer edge of the shoulder, neck, head, and arms. This is the boundary of *positive space*, foreground, her body. The inner solid line shows the shape that her body encloses. The space within this latter curve is negative space, background. These two shapes are almost identical. One is essentially a scaled mirror image of the other.

Observe that this means that there is a correspondence between the extrema on one shape and the extrema on the other, as follows:

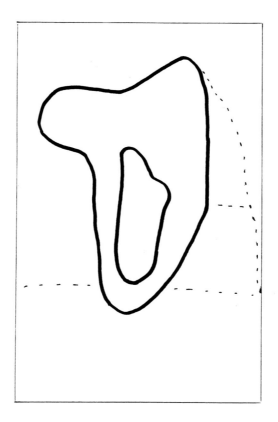

Figure 2.15: Outer and inner shape in Picasso's *Woman Ironing*.

OUTER SHAPE	$\longleftrightarrow$	INNER SHAPE
shoulder	$\longleftrightarrow$	armpit
neck	$\longleftrightarrow$	breast
head	$\longleftrightarrow$	waist
lower hand-line	$\longleftrightarrow$	upper hand-line

This correspondence is crucial to the way Picasso achieves the emotional expressiveness of the work. In order to understand this, we need to understand carefully how the correspondence works in terms of the historical characteristics involved. This is because, according to our theory, the emotional expression is the recovered history.

First observe that the basis of the above correspondence is the Duality Operator. The reason is this: Since the outer shape encloses positive space, and the inner shape encloses negative space, one goes from the outer shape to the inner shape by reversing foreground and background. This, of course, is what the Duality Operator accomplishes.

In order to illustrate the issue of emotional expression, let us take a particular extremum, the *shoulder*, on the outer shape, and its corresponding extremum, the *armpit*, on the inner shape:

First find these two extrema in the list of four in Fig 2.13 p65. Observe that the shading in Fig 2.13 now represents the woman's body, the positive space; and the non-shading represents the background behind the woman. With this in mind, one can easily see that the shoulder is an example of M^+, and the armpit is an example of m^-.

Shoulder M^+
Armpit m^-

Now M^+ is converted into m^- via the Duality Operator. That is, the shoulder and armpit are duals of each other. Recall that, when converting an extremum into its dual, the Duality Operator preserves the first four historical characteristics. This preservation acts as an important means of *unification* across positive and negative space.

Thus, returning to the painting, we observe that the first four historical characteristics of the shoulder must be the same as the first four historical characteristics of the armpit. These characteristics are:

1. Action on recipient space: penetrative
2. Action on extremum point: sharpening
3. Action on surrounding curve: tightening
4. Action in relation to arching: facilitative

Because each of these is a characteristic of the history recovered from the extremum, and because emotional expression is recovered history, each of these is a characteristic of the emotion expressed by the two extrema, as follows:

First characteristic: Whether one considers the shoulder or the armpit, the penetrative nature of these two extrema conveys the fact that both the woman and the environment are intrusions on each other.

Second characteristic: The sharpening nature of these extrema conveys the fact that the woman and the environment are each piercing each other. The scene is a set of *blades* uncomfortably pitched against each other.

Third characteristic: The tightening nature of the curve surrounding each extremum indicates the fact that a process of constriction is going on here.

Fourth characteristic: The facilitative effect on the arching is a subtle emotional effect, in which any penetrative extremum is experienced as involving a quickening effect along its axis – somewhat like an entering sword – in contrast to the slower, turgid, piling, effect that occurs at a compressive extremum.

Thus we see that the first four characteristics allow the artist to set up the same emotional effects in the shoulder as in the armpit. This means that the artist establishes emotional unity, across the two extrema.

However, when turning to the fifth and sixth characteristics, we find that opposite emotional messages are carried at the two extrema. These two characteristics are as follows:

5. Action in relation to positive space
   shoulder = outward
   armpit = inward.
6. Process type

   shoulder = protrusion
   armpit = indentation.

The fifth characteristic, action in relation to positive space, means action in relation to the woman. With respect to this characteristic, the shoulder is outward, and the armpit is inward. Thus the shoulder represents the outward action of the woman, *her attempt to assert self against the environment.* This is clearly conveyed when looking at this extremum in the painting.

In contrast, the armpit, being inward, represents her violation, the encroachment of the environment on her, the destruction of her will, the collapse of self. This again is clearly conveyed when looking at this extremum in the painting.

In the sixth characteristic, the two extrema also differ. The shoulder is the process-type called a *protrusion*. Clearly, an important aspect of the emotional role of the shoulder is based on a sense that it is protruding – with all the consequences of this – e.g., protrusions are obtrusive, they get in the way, they can be knocked and damaged by passing objects, etc. Obviously, this is how the woman has been made to feel about herself – that she is obtrusive, gets in the way, is vulnerable to be knocked and damaged by passing objects, and so on.

In contrast, the armpit is the process-type called an *indentation*. Indentations are not like protrusions. For example, indentations do not obtrude, do not get in the way, etc. They are regions within which things can enter and get stuck. Thus one cannot exchange the concept of indentation for that of protrusion. They are each unique to their respective extremum, and this is due to the particular arrangement of positive and negative space at the extremum.

Let us now understand what has been done above. A crucial devise has been formulated which all great painters use and exploit in the integration of a painting: The artist sets up correspondences between extrema in positive and negative shapes. What provides this correspondence is the Duality Operator. The operator converts each extremum in a positive shape into its foreground-background reversal, its dual, in a negative shape. We have discovered that, under its action, the Duality Operator transfers four of the historical characteristics from an extremum to its dual. This allows unity, integration, to occur across positive and negative space: unity that is both structural and emotional. However, we have also seen that the Duality Operator changes two of the historical characteristics, and this makes the unity non-trivial. That is, unification occurs across two recognizably different extrema. This unity creates a toughness to the canvas exactly because it binds two very different kinds of entities, foreground and background: Foreground is always nearer than background. Foreground advances; background recedes. Yet, by the process of unification, these two separated spaces are pulled together into the single plane of the painting.

This gives the canvas a compacted taut feeling that almost wants to break apart with the pressure of holding, side by side, these two opposite spaces.

All great artists create this crucial almost suffocating tautness, whether Giotto or Cézanne. We shall see later in this series of books that this tautness is an essential component of the world as experienced by a genius – and follows directly from the role of the genius as a unifier. Furthermore, we shall rigorously define what tautness is, as opposed simply to tension. Tautness is the *stabilization* of tension that occurs when unification has been achieved.

For a genius, positive and negative space, although different, are equally important. In importance, nothing stands forward or backward. Nothing is rejected, all is highlighted, all expressive. The spaces between objects are seen as caged animals of emotion as much as the objects that surround them, and participate with the latter equally. Everything speaks with one's mind.

Chapter 3

The Evolution Laws

3.1   Introduction

This chapter develops a set of rules that are the most significant part of our theory of curvature extrema. After developing them, we will be able to analyze the structure of artworks to a new level of expressive power.

To understand what the rules concern, let us go back to the three basic rules that are the foundation of the curvature theory:

> (1) The Symmetry-Curvature Duality Theorem: This says that each curvature extremum has a unique axis leading to, and terminating at, the extremum.

> (2) A particular version of the Symmetry Principle, called the Interaction Principle: This says that the processes, which created the shape, went along symmetry axes.

> (3) A particular use of the Asymmetry Principle: This use says that differences in curvature must be removed backwards in time.

The new rules to be developed are, in fact, a way of more fully understanding the *third rule*, which is an example of the Asymmetry Principle. The general statement of the Asymmetry Principle is that an asymmetry in the present goes back to a symmetry in the past. The asymmetry being considered here is distinguishability in curvature – a distinguishability represented by the *curvature extrema*. We saw that the Asymmetry Principle implies that the curvature extrema in the present shape are removed backward in time, leaving a past shape without curvature extrema. Therefore, in the forward time direction (from past to present), the Asymmetry Principle implies that the process-history successively introduced the curvature extrema.

The rules to be developed, in this chapter, have the purpose of giving a much more detailed map of the process-history than has been given so far. Since the Fundamental Law of Expression, proposed on page 43, says that emotional expression is recovered history, this additional historical information will give deeper insight into the emotional expression of the artwork.

This additional information will be as follows: We have, so far, understood the history to be one of increasing extrema. However, we do not yet have a map of the order in which these extrema accumulated in the shape. For example, consider any particular shape on p26. Some extrema on the shape might have appeared earlier than others; some might have allowed others to appear, and so on. The new rules will infer this extra historical information from any shape. These rules will be called the Extrema Evolution Laws.

EXTREMA EVOLUTION LAWS

The Extrema Evolution Laws express any history of shape evolution in terms of the progressive changes of extrema along that history.

The strategy to be used to develop these laws will be as follows: First, we will use the Asymmetry Principle. This requires that, at any previous stage, there must have been less variation in curvature around the curve, i.e., fewer curvature extrema. Thus, we will select any previous stage, a stage with fewer curvature extrema. Then, given this previous stage, we will consider what happens at the extrema, when time moves forward at the extrema. Note that each extremum already has its own process, going along its symmetry axis, and terminating at that extremum. Our concern will be with what happens when this process continues pushing the boundary further at the extremum. The two alternative cases we must examine are:

(1) **Continuation:** The process simply continues along the axis, maintaining that single axis.

(2) **Bifurcation:** The process branches into two axes, i.e., creating two processes out of one.

Now, because there are four types of extrema, it is necessary to look at what happens when one continues the process at each of the four types, and at what happens when one branches (bifurcates) the process at each of the four types. This means that there are *eight* types of evolutions that can occur at extrema: four continuations and four bifurcations. In fact, as we shall see, in two of these eight evolutions, nothing actually happens; i.e., they are structurally trivial. This leaves a total of six actual evolutions. They will be called the Extrema-Evolution Laws, or simply the Evolution Laws. I invented them in the 1980s and published them in Leyton [14]. They have since been applied in several disciplines such as meteorology, radiology, chemical engineering, computer-aided design, geology, etc. Together, these six laws constitute a system I call the *Process-Grammar*. In this chapter, we shall see that they give enormous insight into the structure and meaning of paintings.

Once again, this opposes the common view that the emotional expression of a painting is undefinable. The Process-Grammar makes the structure and emotional content of a painting rigorously and systematically definable. Furthermore, in doing so, it reveals the emotional content to a far greater level than has previously been possible in the history of art.

3.2   Process Continuations

We start by considering continuations, and later turn to bifurcations. There are four extrema, as listed in this table:

EXTREMUM TYPE	$\longleftrightarrow$	PROCESS TYPE
M^+	$\longleftrightarrow$	protrusion
m^-	$\longleftrightarrow$	indentation
m^+	$\longleftrightarrow$	squashing
M^-	$\longleftrightarrow$	resistance

Here, each extremum is shown together with the type of process that occurs at that extremum. The process-type is in fact the sixth historical characteristic, and this characteristic has been isolated by the table, because it is a very useful way of recognizing extrema in diagrams, as will be seen.

We are simply going to go through the four extrema, as listed in this table, and see what happens at each one, when the process is continued forward in time.

3.3   Continuation at M^+ and m^-

It turns out that, when one continues the process at either of the first two extrema, M^+ or m^-, nothing significant happens. These are the two trivial cases mentioned earlier.

To see this, first consider continuation at M^+. The shape in Fig 3.1 contains three examples of M^+. In accord with the above table, each of these three corresponds to a *protrusion*.

We want to consider what happens when any one of the M^+ processes is continued. For example, consider the bottom M^+ extremum. What happens when the protruding process, which created this extremum, pushes the boundary further along the direction of the arrow? It is clear that the boundary would remain a M^+ extremum, even though it would be pushed down further. This is no more than saying that a protrusion remains a protrusion if it continues. Thus, from now on, continuation at M^+ will be ignored as structurally trivial. Nothing actually changes in terms of extrema.

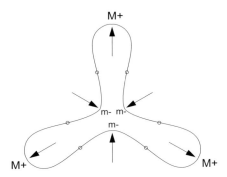

Figure 3.1: Continuation at M^+ and m^- do not change extremum-type.

Exactly the same is true of continuation at a m^- extremum, as can be illustrated by looking at the same shape, Fig 3.1. Notice that there are three m^- extrema on this shape. In accord with the above table, each of these corresponds to an *indentation*. It is clear that, if the process continues at a m^-, the boundary would remain m^-. This is no more than saying that an indentation remains an indentation if it continues. Thus, from now on, continuation at m^- will also be ignored as structurally trivial.

The above two cases, continuation at M^+ and at m^-, are the only two cases that are structurally trivial in terms of extrema. All the remaining cases are non-trivial and will be shown to be fundamentally important in the analysis of artworks. Let us therefore consider them carefully:

3.4   Continuation at m^+

It is necessary to investigate what happens when the process at a m^+ extremum is continued forward in time. To do this, consider the m^+ at the top of the left shape in Fig 3.2. The process at this extremum is a squashing. That is, the process explains the flattening that occurs at the extremum, relative to the sharpness at either end of the top. The fact that this central process is a squashing conforms to the table on p75 which says that a m^+ extremum always corresponds to a squashing.

The question which will concern us is this: What happens when the process at this m^+ extremum is continued forward in time? The answer is shown in the transition from the left shape to the right shape: The process has caused an indentation.

For our analyses of artworks, it is crucial to understand this change carefully in terms of the extrema involved. First, the m^+ at the top of the left shape changes into the m^- at the top of the right shape. The correspondence, in the table on p75, correctly predicts that the process at this m^- is an indentation.

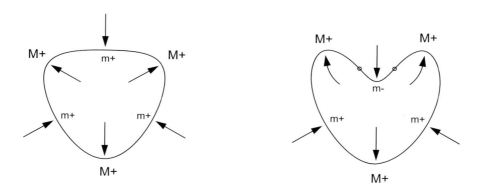

Figure 3.2: Continuation at m^+.

One other thing needs to be observed: On either side of the m^- extremum, at the top of the right shape, there is a small circular dot. A dot marks a place where the curvature is zero. That is, if one were driving around this curve, then the dot would mark the place where the steering wheel would point straight ahead. This only happens briefly, but it does occur, and it occurs exactly at the two dots shown.

Thus we can describe exactly what has happened in the transition from the left shape to the right shape: The m^+ extremum at the top of the left shape has changed into a m^- extremum at the top of the right shape, and two points of zero curvature (flatness) have been introduced on either side of the m^-.

The top of the right shape can therefore be represented as a *triple* of crucial points: the central m^- extremum together with the two points of zero curvature, 0, on either side. This triple can be written thus:

$$0m^-0.$$

Therefore the transition from the left shape to the right shape can be described by saying that the m^+ in the left shape has been replaced by the triple, $0m^-0$, in the right shape. We can write this transition thus:

$$m^+ \longrightarrow 0m^-0.$$

This transition will be labeled as follows:

$$Cm^+$$

which reads: Continuation at m^+.

Putting the above transition, $m^+ \longrightarrow 0m^-0$, together with its label, Cm^+, one obtains this:

$$Cm^+ \;:\; m^+ \;\longrightarrow\; 0m^-0.$$

Reading this sequence of symbols, one by one, from left to right, it says:

Continuation at m^+, takes m^+ and replaces it by the triple $0m^-0$.

When needed, a simple phrase will be used to summarize what happens in the transition, thus: Since the extremum m^+ in the left shape is a squashing, and the extremum m^- in the right shape is an indentation, then our "short-hand" phrase describing the change will be this:

A squashing continues till it indents.

Let us now understand this transition in terms of the historical characteristics involved. These will give the expressive role of the transition, as will be seen in our analyses of paintings.

Recall that each extremum has six historical characteristics. Since the above transition involves a change from one extremum to another, it must involve a change from the six characteristics of one extremum to the six characteristics of the other. Since each historical characteristic is an emotional characteristic of the extremum, the transition must be a change from the six emotional characteristics of one extremum into the six emotional characteristics of the other.

Let us now go through the six characteristics in turn, showing what the above transition does to each of them:

(1) Action on recipient space. The recipient space is the space towards which the process-arrow points. In the case we are considering, illustrated in Fig 3.2, the recipient space is that enclosed by the curve. As can be seen clearly in this diagram, the m^+ process on the left shape is *compressive*. In contrast, the m^- process on the right shape is *penetrative*. It has actually entered the body of the shape. Thus one can see that, in the transition from the left shape to the right shape, the process changes from being a compressive one to being a penetrative one.

(2) Action on extremum point. As observed previously, the m^+ process on the left shape has a *flattening* effect at the extremum. This contrasts with the m^- process on the right shape, which has a *sharpening* effect at the extremum, i.e., it makes the curve more bent. Thus one sees that, in the transition from the left shape to the right shape, the process changes from being a flattening one to being a sharpening one.

(3) Action on surrounding curve. In the left shape, the m^+ process *broadens* the curve surrounding the extremum. That is, the curve on either side of the extremum is pushed apart (it starts as a circle). In contrast, the m^- process on the right shape *tightens* its surrounding curve. That is, the curve on either side of the extremum is pulled together. Thus one sees that, in the transition from the left shape to the right shape, the process changes from having a broadening effect to having a tightening effect.

(4) Relation of action to arching. Now consider the relation of the process to the arching of the curve. In the left shape, the arch of the curve points (slightly) up at the

m^+ extremum. However, the process at that extremum, points down. Thus the process is *oppositional* to the arching. In contrast, in the right shape, the arch of the curve points down at the m^- extremum, while the process also points down. This means that the process is actually *facilitative* to the arching. In conclusion, one sees that, in the transition from the left shape to the right shape, the process changes from being an oppositional one to being a facilitative one.

(5) **Relation of action to positive space.** The positive space, in both the left and right shapes, is the space enclosed by the curve. As can be seen clearly from Fig 3.2, the m^+ process on the left shape points in the *inward* direction to the positive space. This is also true of the m^- process on the right shape. Thus one sees that, in the transition from the left shape to the right shape, there is no change in the inward direction of the process.

(6) **Process-type.** As documented earlier, the m^+ process on the left shape is a *squashing*. In contrast, the m^- process on the right shape is an *indentation*. Therefore, in the transition from the left shape to the right shape, the process changes from a squashing to an indentation.

This concludes our discussion of the first kind of transition that can happen between shapes at their extrema. This transition is our first Evolution Law. It says that continuation at m^+, replaces m^+ by the triple $0m^-0$. The law will be used several times in this book to reveal the expressive force of a painting.

3.5 Continuation at M^-

Recall that we are going through each of the four extrema in turn, describing what happens when the process at the extremum is allowed to continue forward in time. With respect to the first two extrema, M^+ and m^-, it was found that nothing structurally happens, and therefore these two cases were rejected as trivial. However, we have just studied the third extremum m^+ and found that, in this case, there is a significant change when the process is allowed to continue.

We come now to the fourth and final extremum, M^-. Recall that an example of this extremum was encountered when we studied a bay, which is shown again in the left shape in Fig 3.3. That is, the left shape can be regarded as showing the coast-line of an island in the ocean. In the upper half of this island, one can see a bay.

Let us recall the standard way in which a bay is formed, using this island as an example. The island itself was initially circular. At some point in time, there was an inflow of water at the top part of the coast-line. Therefore, that part of the coast-line started to dip inwards. However, as the water continued to go further into the island, it eventually encountered a ridge of mountains, along the central horizontal line of the island. The ridge acted as a resistance against the water flowing further in this direction. Thus the water started to bulge out on either side, and the bay began to form. This lead to the left shape shown in Fig 3.3.

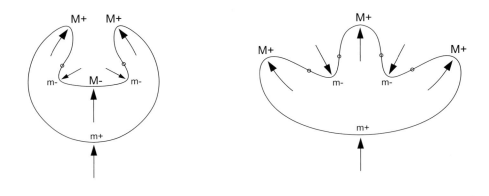

Figure 3.3: Continuation at M^-.

In the bay, one can see that the central point is the extremum M^-, the flattest point. This flattening was caused by the resistance of the mountains. And, below the M^-, there is an upward arrow leading to the M^-, indicating this resisting effect. With respect to this phenomenon, recall the correspondence between curvature extremum and process-type, given in the table on p75. According to this table, the fourth extremum, M^-, always corresponds to the process of resistance. This is clearly evidenced in the example of the bay.

Now we turn to the main issue of this section: What happens when this upward resistive force is continued along the direction of the arrow. How could this possibly happen in the island? The answer is simple: Imagine that, in the mountains, there is a volcano. This volcano erupts, sending lava down into the sea. The result would therefore be the shape shown on the right of Fig 3.3. That is, a promontory would be formed out into the sea.

We will now understand this change carefully in terms of the extrema involved. First, the M^- in the bay in the left shape changes to the M^+ at the top of the right shape. The correspondence, given in the table on p75, correctly predicts that the process at the M^+ in the right shape is a protrusion.

One other thing needs to be observed. On either side of the M^+ extremum, at the top of the right shape, there is a dot. As noted earlier, a dot marks a place where the curvature is zero. That is, if one were driving around this curve, then the dot would mark the place where the steering wheel would point straight ahead. This happens at the two dots shown.

Thus we can describe what has happened in the transition from the left shape to the right shape: The M^- extremum in the bay of the left shape has changed into a M^+ extremum at the top of the right shape, and two points of zero curvature have been introduced on either side of the M^+.

The top of the right shape can therefore be represented as a *triple* of crucial points: the central M^+ extremum together with the two points of zero curvature, 0, on either side. This triple can be written thus:

$$0M^+0.$$

The reader might notice two additional dots slightly further down the protrusion in the right shape. However, these two dots already existed in the island, as shown on the left. They can actually be seen on the two sides of the bay. Since they are neither added nor taken away in the transition from the left shape to the right shape, it is not necessary to consider them in defining the transition.

Therefore the transition can be described by saying that the M^- in the center of the bay in the left shape has been replaced by the triple, $0M^+0$, at the very top of the right shape. We can write the transition as follows:

$$M^- \longrightarrow 0M^+0.$$

This transition will be labeled

$$CM^-$$

which reads: Continuation at M^-.

Putting the above transition, $M^- \longrightarrow 0M^+0$, together with its label, CM^-, one obtains this:

$$CM^- \; : \; M^- \longrightarrow 0M^+0.$$

Reading this sequence of symbols, one by one, from left to right, it says:

Continuation at M^-, takes M^- and replaces it by the triple $0M^+0$.

When needed, a simple phrase will be used to summarize what happens in the transition, as follows: Since the extremum M^- in the left shape is a resistance, and the extremum M^+ in the right shape is a protrusion, our "short-hand" phrase describing the change will be this:

A resistance continues till it protrudes.

Let us now understand this transition in terms of the historical characteristics involved. These will give the expressive role of this transition, as will be seen several times in our analyses of paintings. Each extremum has six historical characteristics. Since the above transition involves a change from one extremum to another, it must involve a change from the six characteristics of one extremum to the six characteristics of the other, as follows:

(1) Action on recipient space. The recipient space is the space towards which the process-arrow points. In the case we are considering, illustrated in Fig 3.3, the recipient space is the ocean of water that surrounds the island. That is, in both the left and right shape, the arrow under consideration points out towards the water. As can be seen clearly in the diagram, the M^- process in the bay in the left shape is *compressive* against the inflow of water. In contrast, the M^+ process on the right shape is *penetrative*. It has actually entered the ocean of water. Thus one sees that, in the transition from the left shape to the right shape, the process changes from being a compressive one to being a penetrative one.

(2) Action on extremum point. As observed previously, the upward M^- process on the left shape has a *flattening* effect at the extremum. This contrasts with the M^+ process on the right shape, which has a *sharpening* effect at the extremum, i.e., it makes the curve more bent. Thus one sees that, in the transition from the left shape to the right shape, the process changes from being a flattening one to being a sharpening one.

(3) Action on surrounding curve. In the left shape, the upward M^- process *broadens* the surrounding curve. That is, the curve on either side of the extremum is pushed apart. In contrast, the M^+ process on the right shape *tightens* its surrounding curve. That is, the curve on either side of the extremum is pulled together. Thus one sees that, in the transition from the left shape to the right shape, the process changes from having a broadening effect to having a tightening effect.

(4) Relation of action to arching. In the left shape, the arch of the bay points down at the M^- extremum. However, the process at that extremum, points up. Thus the process is *oppositional* to the arching. In contrast, in the right shape, the arch of the curve points up at the M^+ extremum while the process also points up. This means that the process is actually *facilitative* to the arching. In conclusion, one sees that, in the transition from the left shape to the right shape, the process changes from being oppositional to facilitative.

(5) Relation of action to positive space. The positive space, in both the left and right shapes, is the space enclosed by the curve. As can be seen from Fig 3.3, the upward M^- process on the left shape points in the *outward* direction from the positive space. This is also true of the M^+ process on the right shape. Thus one sees that, in the transition from the left shape to the right shape, there is no change in the outward direction of the process.

(6) Process-type. As we have documented already, the M^- process on the left shape is a *resistance*. In contrast, the M^+ process on the right shape is a *protrusion*. Thus, in the transition from the left shape to the right shape, the process changes from being a resistance to being an protrusion.

This concludes our discussion of continuation at the fourth extremum, M^-. Of the four extrema, continuation only at m^+ and at M^+ were structurally non-trivial. The continuation at m^+ defined our first Evolution Law. The continuation we have just discussed, that at M^-, defines our second Evolution Law. It says that continuation at M^-, replaces M^- by the triple $0M^+0$. This was the final continuation that we had to consider.

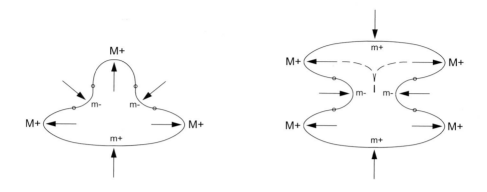

Figure 3.4: Bifurcation at M^+.

3.6 Bifurcations

Recall that we are examining what happens, at an extremum, when one moves time forward; i.e., when the process is allowed to *push the boundary further*.

The above sections investigated what happens when a process simply *continues* along the direction of its axis. We now turn to what happens when a process *bifurcates* (branches) at its extremum. When this investigation is finished, we will have completely classified all the events that can happen when a process moves forward in time at an extremum. These events are crucial in the analysis of artworks, as will be seen immediately afterwards, when we do analyses of paintings as different as works by Holbein, Gauguin, Memling, and Picasso.

3.7 Bifurcation at M^+

We first investigate what happens when the process at a M^+ extremum branches. To do this, consider the M^+ at the top of the left shape in Fig 3.4.

The process at this extremum is a protrusion. This fact conforms to the correspondence between extremum and process-type, shown in the table on p75.

The question which will concern us is this: What happens to the left shape in Fig 3.4, when the process at the M^+ extremum branches, as it progresses forward in time? The answer is shown in the right shape. One branch goes to the left, and the other goes to the right.

Once again, it is necessary to understand this change carefully in terms of the extrema involved. Consider the right shape. The first thing to observe is that the extrema, at the ends of the two branches, are both M^+. That is, they are both copies of the original extremum M^+ at the top of the left shape. Thus, what has happened is that the M^+ in the top of the left shape has branched to become two copies of itself in the right shape.

One other thing needs to be observed. In the center of the top of the right shape, a new extremum has been introduced, a m^+ extremum. Observe that the process at this extremum is a *squashing*, as predicted in the table on p75. In fact, this process explains the flattening in the middle of the top, relative to the sharpening towards either end of the top.

Thus it is possible to describe exactly what has happened in the transition from the left shape to the right shape: The M^+ extremum at the top of the left shape has changed into two copies of itself in the top of the right shape, and a single m^+ extremum has been introduced between them.

The entire top of the right shape can therefore be represented as a *triple* of extrema: the two copies of M^+ on each side, together with the central m^+ extremum between them. This triple can be written thus:

$$M^+ m^+ M^+.$$

Therefore the transition from the left shape to the right shape can be described by saying that the M^+ in the left shape has been replaced by the triple, $M^+ m^+ M^+$, in the right shape. We can write this as follows:

$$M^+ \longrightarrow M^+ m^+ M^+.$$

This transition can be given the following label:

$$BM^+$$

which reads: Bifurcation at M^+.

Putting the above transition, $M^+ \longrightarrow M^+ m^+ M^+$, together with its label, BM^+, one gets this:

$$BM^+ \ : \ M^+ \longrightarrow M^+ m^+ M^+.$$

Reading this sequence of symbols, one by one, from left to right, it says:

Bifurcation at M^+ takes M^+ and replaces it by the triple $M^+ m^+ M^+$.

When needed, a simple phrase will be used to summarize what happens in the transition, as follows: Note that the top structure of the right shape seems to have widened for the purpose of creating a protective front, shielding the lower structure from the downward squashing that has appeared from above. Thus, this top surface will be described simply as a *shield*. This leads us to summarize the *transition*, from the left to right shape, in the following way:

Shield-formation.

Notice that a shield is the figure-ground reversal of a bay.

It is essential, for our later analysis of paintings, to understand this transition in terms of the historical characteristics involved. These give the expressive role of the transition. Since the starting extremum on the left shape is the same as the two outer extrema which it creates on the right shape, it is worthwhile concentrating here on the transition, from the extremum on the left shape, to the *central* extremum on the right shape. Let us go through the six historical characteristics in turn, showing what that transition does to each of the characteristics:

(1) Action on recipient space. The recipient space is always the space towards which the process-arrow points. With respect to the M^+ process at the top of the left shape, the recipient space is the space outside the closed curve. As can clearly be seen, the M^+ process is *penetrative*. It invades the outside space. In contrast, the recipient space for the central m^+ process, on the top of the right shape, is the space within the closed curve. This means that the m^+ process is *compressive*. It squashes down the shape. Thus we see that, in the transition from the left shape to the right shape, the central process changes from being a penetrative one to being a compressive one.

(2) Action on extremum point. The effect of the M^+ process, at the top of the left shape, is to create greater bend at the extremum point, i.e., create a *sharpening* at the extremum. In contrast, the m^+ process on the top of the right shape has a *flattening* effect at the extremum. Thus we see that, in the transition from the left shape to the right shape, the process at the center changes from being a sharpening one to being a flattening one.

(3) Action on surrounding curve. In the left shape, observe the effect of the M^+ process on the curve surrounding the extremum. The effect is that of *tightening* the curve. That is, the curve on either side of the extremum is pulled together, towards the central process-arrow. In contrast, consider the central m^+ process on the top of the right shape. This has a *broadening* or opening effect on the curve. That is, the curve on either side of this extremum is pushed apart. Thus we see that, in the transition from the left shape to the right shape, the process at the center changes from having a tightening effect to having a broadening effect.

(4) Relation of action to arching. In the left shape, the arch of the curve points up at the central M^+ extremum. Furthermore, the process at that extremum also points up. Thus the process is *facilitative* to the arching. In contrast, in the right shape, the arch of the curve also points up at the m^+ extremum, whereas the process points down at this extremum. This means that the process is actually *oppositional* to the arching. In conclusion, we see that, in the transition from the left shape to the right shape, the process at the center changes from facilitative to oppositional.

(5) Relation of action to positive space. The positive space, for both the left and right shapes, is the space enclosed by the curve. Now, as can be seen from Fig 3.4, the M^+ process on the left shape points in the *outward* direction from the positive space. This contrasts with the central m^+ process on the top of the right shape, which points *inward* relative to the positive space. Thus we see that, in the transition from the left shape to the right shape, the process at the center changes from outward to inward.

(6) Process-type. As was documented already, the M^+ process on the left shape is a *protrusion*. In contrast, the m^+ process on the right shape is a *squashing*. Thus, in the

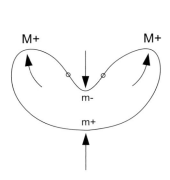 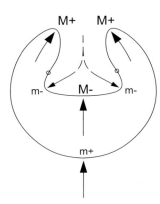

Figure 3.5: Bifurcation at m^-.

transition from the left shape to the right shape, the process at the center changes from a protrusion to a squashing.

This concludes our discussion of the first kind of branching that can happen at an extremum. This transition is one of our Evolution Laws. It says that bifurcation, at M^+, replaces M^+ by the triple $M^+m^+M^+$. This law will be used many times in this book to analyze the expressive force of a painting.

3.8   Bifurcation at m^-

Let us now investigate what happens when the process at a m^- extremum branches. To do this, consider the m^- in the center of the left shape in Fig 3.5. The process at this extremum is an *indentation*, as predicted by the table on p75.

We now ask what happens to the left shape in Fig 3.5, when the process at the m^- extremum branches, as it progresses forward in time. The answer is shown in the transition from the left shape to the right shape: One branch of the process goes to the left, and the other goes to the right.

The consequence is the formation of a bay!

Previously, when discussing the bay, the right diagram was presented without its preceding history (i.e., the left shape). However, we now need to understand this history rigorously, because it will be essential for analyzing the emotional expressiveness of several paintings, e.g., of Holbein and Gauguin.

The first thing to do is examine the history carefully in terms of the extrema involved.

Consider the right shape. Observe that, as established in our earlier study of the bay (p58-63), the extrema, at the ends of the two branches are each m^-. However, what should now be understood is this:

The two m^- extrema, at either end of the bay, are in fact copies of a single m^- extremum at the preceding historical stage.

Therefore, the m^- in the left shape has *branched* into two copies of itself in the right shape.

Another crucial thing needs to be observed. In the transition from the left to the right shape, a new extremum is introduced: the M^- in the center of the bay on the right. This means that the central M^- extremum, which we saw is so essential to the structure of the bay, is introduced by *bifurcation of m^-*.

It is now possible to rigorously describe the final crucial stage in the formation of the bay, the stage shown by the transition from left to right in Fig 3.5: The m^- extremum in the left shape has changed into two copies of itself in the right shape, and a single M^- extremum has been introduced between them.

The entire bay in the right shape can of course be represented as a *triple* of extrema: the two copies of m^- at each end, together with the central M^- extremum between them, thus:

$$m^- M^- m^-.$$

Therefore the transition from the left to the right shape can be described by saying that the m^- in the left shape has been replaced by the triple, $m^- M^- m^-$, in the right shape. We can write this as follows:

$$m^- \longrightarrow m^- M^- m^-.$$

This transition will be given the following label:

$$Bm^-$$

which reads: Bifurcation at m^-.

Putting the above transition, $m^- \longrightarrow m^- M^- m^-$, together with its label, Bm^-, one gets this:

$$Bm^- : m^- \longrightarrow m^- M^- m^-.$$

Reading this sequence of symbols, one by one, from left to right, it says:

Bifurcation at m^- takes m^- and replaces it by the triple $m^- M^- m^-$.

The transition is the crucial final stage in the formation of a bay.

It is essential, for our later analysis of paintings, to understand this transition in terms of the historical characteristics involved. These give the expressive role of the transition. Since the starting extremum on the left shape is the same as the two outer extrema which it creates on the right shape, it is worthwhile concentrating here on the transition, from the extremum on the left shape, to the *central* extremum on the right shape. Let us go through the six historical characteristics in turn, showing what that transition does to each of the characteristics:

(1) Action on recipient space. The recipient space is always the space towards which the process-arrow points. With respect to the m^- process in the left shape, the recipient space is the space inside the closed curve. As can clearly be seen, the m^- process is *penetrative*. It invades the inside space. In contrast, the recipient space for the central M^- process, in the center of the right shape, is the space outside the closed curve. This means that the M^- process is *compressive*. It compresses the "water" outside the shape. Thus we see that, in the transition from the left shape to the right shape, the process at the center changes from penetrative to compressive.

(2) Action on extremum point. The effect of the m^- process, in the left shape, is to create greater bend at that extremum point, i.e., create a *sharpening* at the extremum. In contrast, the M^- process in the center of the right shape has a *flattening* effect at the extremum. Thus we see that, in the transition from the left shape to the right shape, the process at the center changes from sharpening to flattening.

(3) Action on surrounding curve. In the left shape, the m^- process *tightens* the curve surrounding it. That is, the curve on either side of the extremum is pulled together, towards the central process-arrow. In contrast, the central M^- process, in the right shape, *broadens* or opens its surrounding curve. That is, the curve on either side of this extremum is pushed apart. Thus we see that, in the transition from the left shape to the right shape, the process at the center changes from tightening to broadening.

(4) Relation of action to arching. In the left shape, the arch of the curve points down at the central m^- extremum. Furthermore, the process at that extremum also points down. Thus the process is *facilitative* to the arching. In contrast, in the right shape, the arch of the curve points down at the M^- extremum, while the process points up. This means that the process is actually *oppositional* to the arching. In conclusion, we see that, in the transition from the left shape to the right shape, the process at the center changes from facilitative to oppositional.

(5) Relation of action to positive space. The positive space, for both the left and right shapes, is the space enclosed by the curve. As can be seen from Fig 3.5, the m^- process on the left shape points in the inward direction to the positive space. This contrasts with the central M^- process on the bay of the right shape, which points in an outward direction from the positive space. Thus in the transition from the left shape to the right shape, the process at the center changes from inward to outward.

(6) Process-type. As documented above, the m^- process on the left shape is an *indentation*. In contrast, the M^- process on the right shape is a *resistance*. Thus, in the transition from the left shape to the right shape, the process at the center changes from indentation to resistance.

This concludes our discussion of the second kind of branching that can happen at an extremum. This transition is one of our Evolution Laws. It says that bifurcation, at m^-, replaces m^- by the triple $m^-M^-m^-$. This law will be used several times in the book to analyze the expressive force of a painting.

3.9 The Bifurcation Format

The first two bifurcations have just been completed: Bifurcation at M^+, and Bifurcation at m^-. There are two more bifurcations to describe, and this will complete the Evolution Laws. However, before giving the final two bifurcations, it is worth noting the following: It turns out that all four bifurcations have the same format, which is this:

$$E \longrightarrow EeE.$$

In this format, an extremum E is sent to two copies of itself, and a new extremum e is introduced between the two copies. The new extremum e is determined completely from E as follows: Extremum e must be the opposite type from E. That is, if E is a Maximum (M), then e must be a minimum (m), and vice versa. In addition, extremum e must have the same sign as E, that is, "+" or "−" ("bends out" or "bends in").

To illustrate, consider again Bifurcation at M^+, which we found to be this:

$$M^+ \longrightarrow M^+m^+M^+.$$

It is clear from this, that M^+ is sent to two copies of itself. Furthermore, a new extremum, m^+, is introduced in between, which changes the type, from M to m, but has the same sign, "+".

THE BIFURCATION FORMAT

All four bifurcations have the same format,

$$E \longrightarrow EeE$$

E is sent to two copies of itself with a new extremum e, in between, of the opposite type but the same sign.

Now let us continue with the final two bifurcations, and thus complete the Evolution Laws.

3.10 Bifurcation at m^+

Let us now investigate what happens when the process at a m^+ extremum branches. To do this, consider the m^+ at the top of the ellipse in Fig 3.6. The process at this extremum is a squashing, as predicted by the table on p75.

Now we ask what happens to the left shape in Fig 3.6, when the process at the top m^+ extremum branches, as it progresses forward in time. The answer is shown the right shape as follows:

The two branches or copies of the original m^+ process are now on either side of the right shape, both labeled as m^+. Although the situation looks awkward, it is literally the case that both of these side-processes started as the single process at the top of the left shape. This single process split into two copies, which moved away from each other along the shape, to their positions on the sides of the right shape. One should imagine the processes as *sliding* over the surface till they reached their current positions.

Figure 3.6: Bifurcation at m^+.

Starting at the center, the two copies TRAVELED OUT ALONG THE SURFACE, till they reached their positions on either side of the protrusion in the right shape.

Besides this sliding-around of the two m^+ copies, there is another crucial event. In the top of the right shape, a new extremum has been introduced, M^+. Observe that the upward process here conforms to the table on p75, which says that a M^+ extremum always corresponds to a protrusion.

The entire top of the right shape can therefore be represented as a *triple* of extrema: the two copies of m^+ on each side, together with the central M^+ extremum between them, thus:

$$m^+M^+m^+.$$

Therefore one can represent the transition from the left shape to the right shape by saying that the m^+ in the left shape has been replaced by the triple, $m^+M^+m^+$, in the right shape. We can write this as follows:

$$m^+ \longrightarrow m^+M^+m^+.$$

This transition will be given the following label:

$$Bm^+$$

which reads: Bifurcation at m^+.

Putting the above transition, $m^+ \longrightarrow m^+M^+m^+$, together with its label, Bm^+, one gets this:

$$Bm^+ : m^+ \longrightarrow m^+M^+m^+.$$

Reading this sequence of symbols, one by one, from left to right, it says:

Bifurcation at m^+ takes m^+ and replaces it by the triple $m^+M^+m^+$.

As usual a simple phrase will also be needed to summarize what happens in the transition. The phrase can be constructed as follows: It was observed that, after the splitting of the central squashing process in the left shape, the two copies literally move over the surface of the shape till they reach their positions on either side of the protrusion on the right shape.

One can understand these two copies as *pushed aside* by the new protrusion that is introduced. Thus the protrusion can be thought of as breaking through the squashing process:

There is a breaking-through. The initial squashing process is pushed to either side by the newly inserted protrusion.

This leads us to the single phrase that will be used to summarize this evolution law. The phrase is this;

The breaking-through of a protrusion.

It will be seen later that this description has a deep significance that cannot be imagined at the moment.

Again, for our later analysis of paintings, it is necessary to understand this transition in terms of the historical characteristics involved. These give the expressive role of the transition. Since the starting extremum on the left shape is the same as the two outer extrema which it creates on the right shape, it is worthwhile concentrating here on the transition, from the extremum on the left shape, to the *central* extremum on the right shape. Let us go through the six historical characteristics in turn, showing what that transition does to each of the characteristics:

(1) Action on recipient space. The recipient space is always the space towards which the process-arrow points. With respect to the m^+ process at the top of the left shape, the recipient space is the space inside the closed curve. As can clearly be seen, the m^+ process is *compressive*. In contrast, the recipient space for the central M^+ process, at the top of the right shape, is the space outside the closed curve. This means that the M^+ process is *penetrative*. It invades the outside space. Thus, in the transition from the left shape to the right shape, the process at the center changes from compressive to penetrative.

(2) Action on extremum point. The effect of the m^+ process, at the top of the left shape, is to *flatten* the curve. In contrast, the M^+ process at the top of the right shape has a *sharpening* effect at the extremum; i.e., making it more bent. Thus, in the transition from the left shape to the right shape, the process at the center changes from flattening to sharpening.

(3) Action on surrounding curve. In the left shape, the m^+ process *broadens* the surrounding curve. That is, the curve on either side of the extremum is pushed apart. In contrast, the central M^+ process at the top of the right shape *tightens* the surrounding curve. That is, the curve on either side of this extremum is pulled together, towards the central arrow. Thus, in the transition from the left shape to the right shape, the process at the center changes from broadening to tightening.

(4) Relation of action to arching. In the left shape, the arch of the curve points up at the central m^+ extremum. However, the process at that extremum points down. Thus the process is *oppositional* to the arching. In contrast, in the right shape, the arch of the curve points up at the M^+ extremum, while the process also points up. This means that the process is actually *facilitative* to the arching. The conclusion is that, in the transition from the left shape to the right shape, the process at the center changes from oppositional to facilitative.

(5) Relation of action to positive space. The positive space, for both the left and right shapes, is the space enclosed by the curve. As can be seen from Fig 3.6, the m^+ process on the left shape points in the *inward* direction to the positive space. This contrasts with the central M^+ process at the top of the right shape, which points in an *outward* direction from the positive space. Thus, in the transition from the left shape to the right shape, the process at the center changes from inward to outward.

(6) Process-type. As documented already, the m^+ process on the left shape is a *squashing*. In contrast, the M^+ process on the right shape is a *protrusion*. Thus, in the transition from the left shape to the right shape, the process at the center changes from squashing to protrusion.

This concludes our discussion of the third kind of branching that can happen at an extremum. This transition is one of our Evolution Laws. It says that bifurcation at m^+ replaces m^+ by the triple $m^+M^+m^+$. This law will be used several times in this book to analyze the expressive force of a painting.

3.11   Bifurcation at M^-

We come now to the final Evolution Law: that which describes what happens when the process at a M^- extremum branches. To derive this law, it will be useful to consider the M^- in the center of the bay in Fig 3.7. As we know, the process at this extremum is an internal resistance.

We now ask what happens to the bay when the M^- process branches, as it progresses forward in time. The answer is shown in the right shape, which should be understood as follows:

The first thing to notice is that one gets the *deepened bay* on the right. The two branches or copies of the original M^- process are now on either side of the deepened bay: both labeled as M^-. It is literally the case that both of these side-processes started as the single resistance process in the center of the bay in the left shape. Again, it is crucial to understand that the progression involved a *movement*: After this single process split, its two copies moved away from each other along the curve to their positions on the sides of the right shape.

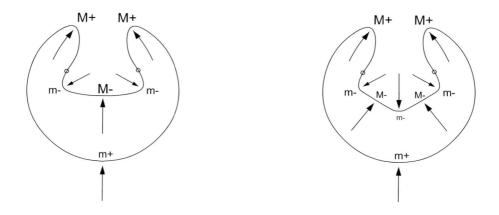

Figure 3.7: Bifurcation at M^-.

Starting at the center, the two copies TRAVELED OUT ALONG THE SURFACE, till they reached their positions on either side of the deepened bay.

Besides this movement, there is another crucial event. In the deepened bay on the right shape, a new extremum has been introduced, the m^-, in the deepest part of the bay. Observe that the downward process at this extremum conforms to the table on p75, which says that m^- always corresponds to an indentation.

Therefore, the entire bottom portion of the deepened bay can be represented as a *triple* of extrema: the two copies of M^- on each side, together with the central m^- extremum between them:

$$M^- m^- M^-.$$

Thus the transition from the left shape to the right shape can be described by saying that the M^- in the left shape has been replaced by the triple, $M^- m^- M^-$, in the right shape:

$$M^- \longrightarrow M^- m^- M^-.$$

This transition will be given the following label:

$$BM^-$$

which reads: Bifurcation at M^-.

Putting the above transition, $M^- \longrightarrow M^- m^- M^-$, together with its label, BM^-, one gets this:

$$BM^- \ : \ M^- \longrightarrow \ M^- m^- M^- .$$

Reading this sequence of symbols, one by one, from left to right, it says:

Bifurcation at M^- takes M^- and replaces it by the triple $M^- m^- M^-$.

As usual a simple phrase will also be needed to summarize what happens in the transition. This phrase can be constructed as follows: It was said that, after the splitting of the central resistance process in the left shape, the two copies literally *move* over the surface of the shape till they reach their positions on either side of the deepened bay in the right shape.

One can understand these two copies as *pushed aside* by the new indentation that is introduced. Thus the indentation can be thought of as breaking through the resistance:

There is a breaking-through. The initial resistance is pushed to either side by the newly inserted indentation.

This leads us to the single phrase that will be used to summarize the evolution law:

The breaking-through of an indentation.

Again, it is essential, for our later analysis of paintings, to understand this transition in terms of the historical characteristics involved. These give the expressive role of the transition. Since the starting extremum on the left shape is the same as the two outer extrema which it creates on the right shape, it is worthwhile concentrating here on the transition, from the extremum on the left shape, to the *central* extremum on the right shape. Let us go through the six historical characteristics in turn, showing what that transition does to each of the characteristics:

(1) Action on recipient space. The recipient space is always the space towards which the process-arrow points. With respect to the M^- process in the center of the bay in the left shape, the recipient space is the space outside of the closed curve, i.e., the "water." As can clearly be seen, the M^- process is *compressive*. It compresses the water. In contrast, the recipient space for the central m^- process, in the right shape, is the space inside the closed curve. This means that the m^- process is *penetrative*. It invades the inside space. Thus, in the transition from the left shape to the right shape, the process at the center changes from compressive to penetrative.

(2) Action on extremum point. The effect of the M^- process, in the center of the bay in the left shape, is to create a *flattening* at the extremum. In contrast, the m^- process in the center of the bay of the right shape has a *sharpening* effect at the extremum; i.e., it creates more bend. Thus, in the transition from the left shape to the right shape, the process at the center changes from flattening to sharpening.

(3) Action on surrounding curve. In the left shape, the central M^- process *broadens* the surrounding curve. That is, the curve on either side of the extremum is pushed apart. In contrast, the central m^- process in the right shape *tightens* its surrounding curve. That is, the curve on either side of this extremum is pulled together, towards the central arrow. Thus, in the transition from the left shape to the right shape, the process at the center changes from broadening to tightening.

(4) Relation of action to arching. In the left shape, the arch of the curve points down at the central M^- extremum. However, the process here points up. Thus the process is *oppositional* to the arching. In contrast, in the right shape, the arch of the curve points down at the central m^- extremum, while the process also points down. This means that the process is *facilitative* to the arching. In conclusion, in the transition from the left shape to the right shape, the process at the center changes from oppositional to facilitative.

(5) Relation of action to positive space. The positive space, for both the left and right shapes, is the space enclosed by the curve. Now observe that the M^- process on the left shape points in the *outward* direction from the positive space. This contrasts with the central m^- process in the bay of the right shape. This points in an *inward* direction to the positive space. Thus, in the transition from the left shape to the right shape, the process at the center changes from outward to inward.

(6) Process-type. As was documented earlier, the M^- process in the left shape is a *resistance*. In contrast, the m^- process on the right shape is an *indentation*. Thus, in the transition from the left shape to the right shape, the process at the center changes from resistance to indentation.

This concludes our discussion of the fourth kind of branching that can happen at an extremum. This transition is the last of our Evolution Laws. It says that bifurcation at M^- replaces M^- by the triple $M^-m^-M^-$. This law will be used very significantly in this book to analyze the expressive force of a painting.

3.12   The Process-Grammar

We have now finished elaborating the Six Evolution Laws. The purpose of these laws is to express the process-history of any shape purely in terms of the progressive changes of curvature extrema, along that history.

The laws were derived by solving the following problem: Given any earlier stage in the history, what happens at the extrema when one runs time forward at the extrema? There are four different extrema to check. And at each extremum, only two alternatives can occur: either a simple continuation, or a bifurcation. This means that there are a total of eight different events that can occur.

However, we found that continuation at the first two extrema, M^+ and m^-, cause no alteration to these extrema, so that we are actually left with a total of six different changes that extrema can undergo in a history. These are the Six Evolution Laws. As noted earlier, I invented these laws in the 1980s and published them in Leyton [14]. They have since been applied by scientists in several disciplines such as *meteorology* by Milios [21], *radiology* by Shemlon [25], *chemical engineering* by Lee [6], *geology* by Larsen [5], Also, in *computer-aided design*, Pernot et al. [22] [23] implemented my six laws as CAD operators for the aerospace/automotive industries.

Together, my six laws constitute a system I call the *Process-Grammar*. The laws are presented together in the next table.

PROCESS-GRAMMAR

$$
\begin{aligned}
Cm^+: & \quad m^+ \longrightarrow 0m^-0 && \text{(squashing continues till it indents)} \\
CM^-: & \quad M^- \longrightarrow 0M^+0 && \text{(resistance continues till it protrudes)} \\
BM^+: & \quad M^+ \longrightarrow M^+m^+M^+ && \text{(sheild-formation)} \\
Bm^-: & \quad m^- \longrightarrow m^-M^-m^- && \text{(bay-formation)} \\
Bm^+: & \quad m^+ \longrightarrow m^+M^+m^+ && \text{(breaking-through of a protrusion)} \\
BM^-: & \quad M^- \longrightarrow M^-m^-M^- && \text{(breaking-through of an indentation)}
\end{aligned}
$$

Observe the following in the table. The first two laws are the two continuations, as can be seen from the fact that the letter C begins the first two lines. In contrast, the last four laws are the bifurcations, as can be seen from the fact that the letter B begins each of these four lines.

Observe also that each of four bifurcations has the format, $E \longrightarrow EeE$. That is, extremum E is sent to two copies of itself with a new extremum e, in between, where e has the opposite type from E (max vs. min) but the same sign.

We now come to an absolutely fundamental concept:

Each of the Six Evolution Laws of the Process-Grammar is an example of the Asymmetry Principle.

That is, each represents an increase in asymmetry over time, as follows:

It is immediately obvious, by direct inspection of the table, that each of the *bifurcations* involves an increase in asymmetry over time, because each begins with a single extremum, to the left of the arrow, and changes this extremum into three extrema, to the right of the arrow. This increase in the number of extrema necessarily involves an increase in the amount of curvature variation – which is the asymmetry we are concerned with here.

Furthermore, a little consideration reveals that the first two laws, the continuations, are also examples of the Asymmetry Principle. This can be illustrated, for instance, by looking at the first law, Cm^+, continuation at m^+, as follows.

Recall that this transition was illustrated by the change from the left shape to the right shape in Fig 3.2. We had asked what happens when one continues the m^+ squashing process, at the top of the left shape, forward in time. The result was that the indentation appears at the top of the right shape. In this transition, the m^+, at the top of the left shape, changes into the triple, $0m^-0$, on the top of the right shape. The two zeros are the two dots on the top of the right shape.

One can easily check that there is more curvature variation in the top of the right shape than the top of the left shape: A car steering wheel would need to change more in driving along the top of the right shape than in driving along the top of the left shape.

The reason is that the curve bends out all along the top of the left shape. However, along the top of the right shape, it oscillates between bending out and in. This oscillation in the right shape is, in fact, due to the presence of the two dots – the two points of zero curvature. Such a point is a place where the curve changes from bending out (+ve) to bending in (-ve). Thus, because the Evolution Law, from the left to right shape

$$m^+ \longrightarrow 0m^-0$$

introduces the zero points, it introduces the oscillation. Since the oscillation is curvature variation, i.e., asymmetry, the law is responsible for introducing an increase in asymmetry.

Exactly the same argument applies to the second continuation law:

$$M^- \longrightarrow 0M^+0$$

That is, because this law also introduces two zero points, it must introduce more oscillation, and hence greater curvature variation, i.e., asymmetry.

The conclusion is that each of the Six Evolution Laws constituting the Process-Grammar is an example of the Asymmetry Principle, i.e., each involves an increase in asymmetry over time. In fact, our discussion actually proved the powerful and extremely important fact that the six laws are the only forms that the Asymmetry Principle can take at curvature extrema.

The Six Evolution Laws of the Process-Grammar are the six possible forms that the Asymmetry Principle can take at curvature extrema.

This fact is very important to our analysis of paintings because it means that the Process-Grammar provides the only six ways that tension can be increased via curvature extrema.

3.13   The Duality Operator and the Process-Grammar

Before continuing, it is necessary to recall the Duality Operator from section 2.7 (p65):

The Duality Operator, D, reverses foreground and background, i.e., it exchanges positive and negative space.

The power of this operator to yield insight into the artwork was illustrated when we applied it to Picasso's *Woman Ironing*. It will be used several times in this book. What reveals so much about the artwork is an examination of how this operator acts on histories – that is, how the operator maps the histories of the positive space onto the histories of the negative space. This issue is crucial because, according to my foundations for geometry, the structure of the artwork is the process-history inferred from the work. The history gives the tension structure. Furthermore, the history is the emotional expression. Now, because the operator sends histories in the positive space to histories in the negative

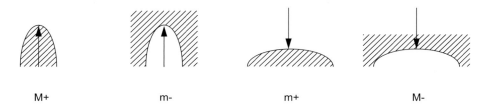

Figure 3.8: The four types of extrema.

space, the operator is basic to unifying the tension in the work. Correspondingly, it unifies the emotional meaning of the painting.

To fully and rigorously define this unification, it is necessary first to recall part of section 2.7, as follows: Fig 3.8 again shows the four extrema. Because the Duality Operator reverses foreground and background, the operator changes the first extremum, into the second, and vice versa. Thus:

$$M^+ \longleftrightarrow m^-$$

Similarly, it changes the third extremum into the fourth, and vice versa. Thus:

$$m^+ \longleftrightarrow M^-$$

Therefore the action of the Duality Operator on curvature extrema is defined in the following way:

Duality Operator, D.

$$M^+ \longleftrightarrow m^- \qquad m^+ \longleftrightarrow M^-$$

Now, as said above, to understand an artwork, one needs to understand the effect of the Duality Operator in mapping the *histories* of the positive space onto the *histories* of the negative space. This means that a deep understanding of painting can come from studying the effect of the Duality Operator on the Six Evolution Laws of Process-Grammar. This is because the Evolution Laws generate the histories.

Thus, to proceed with the analysis, the Six Evolution Laws of the Process-Grammar are given here again:

$$
\begin{aligned}
Cm^+ : &\quad m^+ \longrightarrow 0m^-0 \\
CM^- : &\quad M^- \longrightarrow 0M^+0 \\
BM^+ : &\quad M^+ \longrightarrow M^+m^+M^+ \\
Bm^- : &\quad m^- \longrightarrow m^-M^-m^- \\
Bm^+ : &\quad m^+ \longrightarrow m^+M^+m^+ \\
BM^- : &\quad M^- \longrightarrow M^-m^-M^-
\end{aligned}
$$

Applying the Duality Operator to each of these laws, the following three facts should be observed:

1. When the Duality Operator is applied to the extrema in the first law, the law is converted into the second law, and vice versa.

2. When the Duality Operator is applied to the extrema in the third law, the law is converted into the fourth law, and vice versa.

3. When the Duality Operator is applied to the extrema in the fifth law, the law is converted into the six law, and vice versa.

Thus we are lead to the following conclusion:

> **The Duality Operator divides the Six Evolution Laws of the Process-Grammar into three pairs:**
>
> **[one, two]   [three, four]   [five, six].**
>
> **The Duality operator converts a member of a pair into the other member of that pair.**

With these correspondences established, it now becomes possible to convert the Evolution Laws that the artist used in positive space, into the Evolution Laws used in negative space. This is basic to understanding the structure of the artwork, as we shall see immediately in the next section, when we start to use the Process-Grammar to analyze specific paintings.

3.14   Holbein: *Anne of Cleves*

We will now see that the Process-Grammar gives remarkable insight into the structure, meaning, and emotional expression of paintings. The first painting to be discussed is Holbein's *Anne of Cleves*, shown in Plate 6.

The background to this painting is as follows: Holbein had been sent by Henry VIII to Europe to capture the likeness of Anne, so that Henry would have a chance to inspect his intended bride. The artist's position was not easy. For he had to both please the foreign officials surrounding Anne, but also convey a truthful portrait to Henry, who should not be taken subsequently by surprise if he found Anne displeasing on her arrival in England. Furthermore, the king could also not be insulted should he find her to his liking.

In the end, the competition of these demands was impossible to meet. Henry was horrified by Anne on her arrival – referring to her as a "fat Flanders mare," and Holbein lost much of his prestige with the court.

Anne however was not the bland simpleton that some people have described her to be. In her severe rejection by Henry, she secured a healthy settlement from him, that enabled her to live in solid comfort (in England) for the next fifteen years.

Holbein could see all of this in her character, and the portrait shows to us the quiet complexity of this woman, and her dignified relationship to the circumstances that were about to tragically unfold.

We are now going to see this:

> **Everything that Holbein chooses to express about the woman – her character, her conflicts, her complex set of emotions, the drama of her situation – is expressed as the** *history recoverable from the shape-structure.*

To understand the implications of this, it is first necessary to go back to the basic concepts of my new foundations to geometry: A painting is a frozen structure. There is no actual movement or change on the canvas. However, one of the basic concepts of the new foundations is that an artwork is the process-history recovered from this static structure. Furthermore, my First Fundamental Law of Expression states that emotional expression is recovered history. In fact, what we will see is this:

> **Contrary to the common view that the emotional expression of an artwork is undefinable, the Process-Grammar rigorously and systematically reveals the structure, meaning, and emotional content of Holbein's** *Anne of Cleves.*

Now, the preceding discussion has given my inference rules for inferring history from curvature extrema. The three basic rules define the overall history inferred from the extrema, and the Process-Grammar shows how the history is broken down into successive stages, i.e., the building-blocks out of which the history is constructed.

We shall see that Holbein builds his work out of a three-stage history. Each stage is one of the Evolution Laws. The three successive Evolution Laws that construct the work are as follows:

1. Bay-formation, Bm^-.
2. Bifurcation of resistance, BM^-.
3. Continuation of resistance, CM^-

1. Bay-Formation in *Anne of Cleves*

The first stage, bay-formation, is a significant structural factor in the work. It can be seen in the band of the woman's dress, shown in Fig 3.9.

As was shown earlier, bay-formation involves an opening effect. We see this expressed in the dress-band, which therefore represents the spreading and opening of the woman's inner life.

The bay is so significant that Holbein repeats it as the line of the veil, shown in Fig 3.10. Observe that this veil-line is the same size as the line of the dress-band below it. In fact, the two bays are simply reflectional copies of each other.

Figure 3.9: The bay in the dress-band.

The implied arrows, of bifurcation in the veil, run up her nose and branch across the region of her eyes towards the sides of her forehead. Thus the implied arrows have an *upward*, *opening*, *spreading*, effect on the face – giving it a sense of radiating calm intensity.

It is important to understand the basic theoretical means by which this is achieved: What is being used is the *history* inferred from the line. This is recovered in two stages: First, one uses the three basic rules for the inference of history from curvature extrema. That is, the arrows lie along the symmetry axes leading to the curvature extrema. Second, the two branching arrows are themselves given a history by the Fourth Evolution Law of the Process-Grammar. This law is Bifurcation at m^-

$$m^- \longrightarrow m^- M^- m^-$$

which I call Bay-Formation. That is, the two arrows were, in the past, a single arrow – the symmetry axis of the face – which split and branched to the left and right. The tension between this branched state and the past un-branched state is clearly visible in

Figure 3.10: The bay in the veil.

the face. As my First Fundamental Law of Tension (p11) states: Tension is the use of the Asymmetry Principle; i.e., it occurs from a present asymmetry to its past symmetry. The present asymmetry consists of the two side extrema of the bay, and the past symmetry is the single extremum at the top of the face. The tension goes between the two side extrema and the single extremum. The reader should carefully try to view this.

The Bay-Formation operator yields not only the information just given, but also the following information. For this, it will help the reader to look at Fig 3.11 which shows us again the structure of this operator.

What we will now consider is the creation of the M^- extremum in the center of the bay. Its associated arrow is the central one in Fig 3.11b. As our correspondence between extremum-type and process-type states, this M^- process is a *resistance*.

In this painting, the M^- process represents the resistance of the environment, to the outward action of the woman. Clearly, this embodies the forces of opposition and repression that the woman meets – that were an inevitable part of the enforced restraint of her situation.

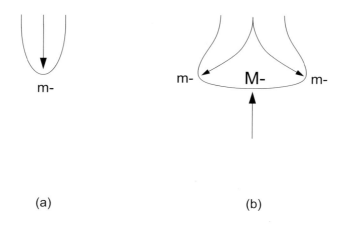

(a)   (b)

Figure 3.11: Bifurcation at m^-.

Thus, consider the M^- extremum in the center of the bay defined by the dress-band. From this extremum, our rules infer the upward resistive force shown in Fig 3.12. In fact, this force is most clearly felt against the outer line of the dress-band. Notice the enormous sense of pressure on this line. The reader is recommended to turn to the actual photograph, Plate 6, and experience this force.

Observe also, that Holbein emphasizes this extremum by the centrally-placed jewel in the dress-band.

The fact that the M^- extremum corresponds to the process of resistance is the sixth historical characteristic, which assigns, to an extremum, its process-type. I have said many times that, because emotional expressiveness is recovered history, the six historical characteristics are the six emotional characteristics of an extremum. This is clearly seen here. Not only does the sixth characteristic, resistance, embody a crucial emotional factor of the situation, but so do the other historical characteristics. For example, the first historical characteristic of M^- is that its inferred process is *compressive*. Obviously, this embodies an important aspect of the emotion being expressed here.

There is a profound reason why the emotions carried by the historical characteristics can be labeled with exactly the same names as we use for the historical characteristics themselves: The historical characteristics correspond to the deformation inferred from the geometry, and the deformation *is* the expression. Notice that facial expressions are deformations of the face; i.e., the expresser deforms shape in order to communicate the expression. Thus, emotionally, the M^- extremum is compressive, flattening, resistive, etc. Clearly, terms like "compressive," "flattening," and "resistive" describe emotional forces in the drama of the situation.

There is another vital fact concerning bay-formation in this work, as follows: In a geographical bay, the negative space is the region corresponding to the water, i.e., the internal region of the bay. Observe from the photograph of the painting (Plate 6)

Figure 3.12: The resistive force against the dress-band.

that the internal region of the bay of the dress-band is indeed experienced as negative space. There are a number of cues that lead the eye to this conclusion. For example, this internal region is background relative to the necklaces and crucifix, which lie over it, and which thus make it visually recede. Also the region surrounding the bay is given a greater substantiality due to its portrayed hardness, robustness, and reflectiveness.

Now, just as Picasso, in *Woman Ironing*, establishes unity across positive and negative space, by ensuring that the shapes of positive space are the foreground-background reversals of those of negative space (and vice versa), Holbein does the same. Thus, elsewhere in the painting, Holbein converts the bay into its foreground-background reversal which he also uses significantly. In the Process-Grammar, the reversal of the bay is the shield, and an important example is shown in Fig 3.13a. It is necessary to carefully understand this structure, as follows:

First let us isolate the top line of the structure. It is the arc shown in Fig 3.13b. This will be called the *shoulder-line*. It is the most dominating line in the painting. Observe that it corresponds to the bottom line of the bay in the dress-band – which can also be

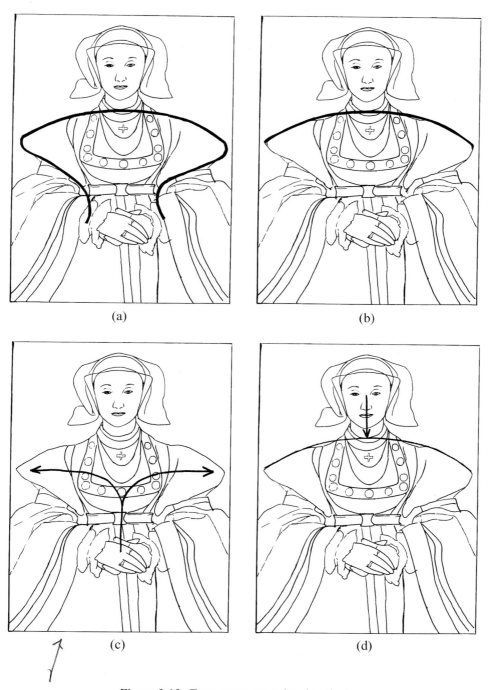

(a)

(b)

(c)

(d)

Figure 3.13: Four structures related to the bay.

BM+
"shield"

seen in this figure. The reader should take a moment to experience the similarity of these two arcs.

However, while the arcs themselves are similar, the foreground-background structure is the opposite. For the dress-band, the region within the arc is negative space, as pointed out earlier. However, for the shoulder, the region within the arc is positive space. This is because the shoulders overlap the background; i.e., Anne is standing in front of the background.

Turn now to the photograph of the painting, Plate 6. From the photograph, one can easily understand why I have called this structure, a shield. The broad arc of the shoulders has a strong defensive role. One can understand this as expressing her situation at the royal court.

Now let us consider how this arc continues: At either end, it turns sharply inwards and sweeps down to her waste – a movement that the artist emphasizes by the large triangular shoulder-pieces, which also dominate the painting. This downward continuation of the shoulder-line was shown in the original diagram, Fig 3.13a.

Now let us turn to the basic issue: the history of the line. This will give the expressive quality. The historical structure is presented in Fig 3.13c and d. Here, Fig 3.13c shows the pair of branching arrows, creating the two side extrema. These convey the outward opening of the woman. Fig 3.13d shows the downward compressive arrow creating the central extremum, which is a m^+. Our sixth historical characteristic states that this extremum always corresponds to a squashing. Clearly, this is the appropriate term for society's action on this woman. The other characteristics are also relevant. They are that a m^+ process is compressive, flattening, broadening, oppositional, and inward.

Notice that the historical characteristics of the m^+ strongly contrast with those of the two side extrema. The latter are both M^+. The six historical characteristics for a M^+ process are penetrative, sharpening, tightening, facilitative, outward, and protruding. These convey the woman's attempt to assert herself upon the environment. Thus the contrast between the historical characteristics of the central m^+ extremum, and the historical characteristics of the two side M^+ extrema, carry the emotional drama of the situation.

The three process-arrows shown in Fig 3.13c and d are each inferred by our three basic rules for the recovery of history from curvature extrema. That is, the arrows lie along the symmetry axes leading to the curvature extrema.

Furthermore, the arrows are themselves given a history by the Third Evolution Law of the Process-Grammar. This law is Bifurcation at M^+

$$M^+ \longrightarrow M^+m^+M^+$$

which we refer to as shield-formation. The law is illustrated in the transition from Fig 3.14a to 3.14b. That is, the law implies that the two branching arrows (Fig 3.14b) were initially a single arrow in the past (Fig 3.14a), which split – one branch going to the left and the other branch going to the right. In addition, the law dictates the production of the central extremum, m^+, which is associated with the downward arrow in Fig 3.14b.

Now consider the crucial issue of *unity*, i.e., integration in the work: The law that has just been described, shield-formation, can be obtained from the law we call bay-formation, by applying the Duality Operator, which reverses negative and positive space.

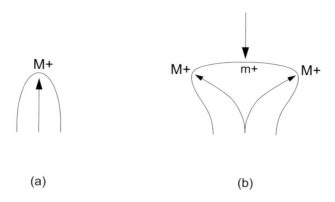

Figure 3.14: Bifurcation at M^+.

Thus one can consider the process-structure in the shoulders as having being transferred to the shoulders from the bay in the dress-band, by the Duality Operator. The two structures are therefore experienced as images of each other. The Duality Operator thus enforces a powerful visual unity in the painting.

2. Bifurcation of resistance in *Anne of Cleves*

We have just been discussing bay-formation (and its dual shield-formation) in Holbein's *Anne of Cleves*. This is the first stage of the three-stage history that occurs in the painting. Let us now move onto the second stage in that history. This is a bifurcation of resistance – which is the Sixth Evolution Law of the Process-Grammar. This law is BM^- described fully in section 3.11. This bifurcation is so important to this painting, that it is necessary first to review the main points of its structure. The reader is strongly recommended to read the six main points listed on p108, before continuing.

We are now ready to return to Holbein's painting.

The most prominent use of the Sixth Evolution Law is shown by the outer bold line in Fig 3.16. The line is the entire shape of her arms. That is, the top ends of the line start at her shoulder joints, emphasized by the slight upward bulges in her clothing. It then descends along the outer edge of her arms, to the elbows, where it turns inward along the arms, and culminates at the linked hands. It is clearly a deepened bay.

The same figure shows the bay of the dress-band, which was studied earlier. This is an ordinary bay and therefore represents the historical stage that precedes the deepened bay. Thus, the progression from the bay of the dress-band to the bay of the arms is exactly the progression from the left shape to the right shape in Fig 3.15.

Figure 3.15: Bifurcation at M^-.

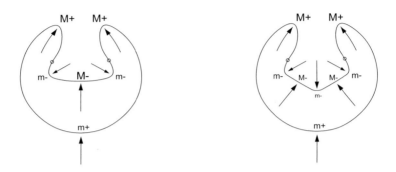

SUMMARY OF BM^-

(1) As shown in the above figure, this bifurcation converts the ordinary bay (left) to the deepened bay (right).
(2) The M^- **extremum on the left shape is split into two copies which** *move away from the center* **of the bay as it deepens, till they reach their positions on the right shape.**
(3) A new extremum m^- **is introduced on the right shape.**
(4) This extremum implies the following description of the bifurcation:

The breaking through of an indentation.

(5) The change in extrema from the left to right shape is:

$$M^- \longrightarrow M^- m^- M^-.$$

(6) Considering only the *central* **extremum of the left and right shape, the changes in historical characteristics are:**

compressive	$\longrightarrow$	penetrative
flattening	$\longrightarrow$	sharpening
broadening	$\longrightarrow$	tightening
oppositional	$\longrightarrow$	facilitative
outward	$\longrightarrow$	inward
resistance	$\longrightarrow$	indentation

Figure 3.16: Deepened bay.

It is worthwhile seeing how the process arrows in Fig 3.15 map to the curves in Fig 3.16. The upward resistance arrow, in the left shape of Fig 3.15, becomes the upward thrust against the bottom line of the dress-band. In the transition to the double-bay of the arms, this resistance process has split into two copies, which are now upward arrows against the center of each forearm. To fully comprehend this, the reader should match the deepened-bay on the right shape in Fig 3.15, to the deepened bay of the arms in Fig 3.16.

It is important to understand that this structure involved movement. Go back to the single initial force at the center of the ordinary bay:

> **After splitting, the two copies** *moved away from the center of the bay as it deepened,* **till they reached their positions against the two lowered forearms.**

What has caused the splitting and subsequent traveling is the introduction of the new downward central process that created the downward vertex at the hands.

Figure 3.17: The veil.

In terms of the expressive qualities that Holbein is trying to convey, one sees that the upward central process against the bottom of the dress-band is *compressive*. In the transition to the deepened bay of the arms, this compressive force is literally pushed aside into the forearms, and is replaced by the downward *penetrative* force at the hands. Thus, in accord with what was said on p108, the new downward penetrative force can be thought of as breaking through the previous upward compressive force:

> **There is a** *breaking-through.* **The central upward compressive force at the dress-band is pushed to either side by a new downward penetrative force at the hands.**

This breaking-through clearly represents the woman's assertion of personal resolve against the restrictive forces of society. One is reminded of the basic role of the concept of breaking-through (durchbruch) in the sermons of the great fourteenth century mystic, Meister Eckhart. Using the concepts of my lectures on psychoanalysis, breaking-through is a giving birth to self, which occurs through a process of self-knowledge. This is clearly the feeling being communicated in the vertex formed at Anne's hands. The downward plunge gives a sense of self-authorship, and the re-assertion of dignity.

Let us now turn from the structure of the arms to the structure of the veil around the face. It was said previously that the veil-line is a reflectional copy of the bay in the dress-band. However, closer inspection reveals that there is a slight difference between these two lines. To see this, consider an enlarged view of the veil, shown in Fig 3.17.

What this version reveals is that the veil has a sharpened extremum at its center. If the veil were an ordinary bay, the center would be the flattest point on the line. In order that the reader can clearly see this, the ordinary bay and the deepened bay are shown again, in Fig 3.18, in the orientation that is relevant for the veil. It is clear that the center of the veil-line in Fig 3.17 does not have the flattened structure of the left shape (ordinary bay) in Fig 3.18, but the pointed structure of the right shape.

Also observe that, if the veil were an ordinary bay, the center would have a *compressive* force that would push downward, as shown in the left shape in Fig 3.18. Instead, the central extremum of the veil has a penetrative force that pushes upward, as shown in the right shape in Fig 3.18.

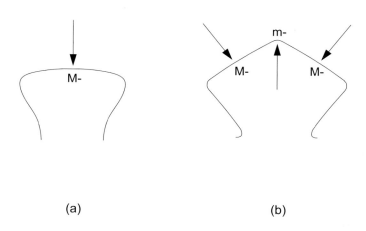

(a)   (b)

Figure 3.18: Bifurcation at M^-.

This latter force carries the sense of breaking through in the Sixth Evolution Law, because it is understood as having caused the sharpening, which means that it has acted on an initially flat curve and sent the flattening to either side.

Thus the artist has carried through the same theme in the veil, as he carried through in the arms. The reader should take time to look again at the line-drawing in Fig 3.16, and try to see the veil-structure and the arm-structure *simultaneously*. This will allow one to experience the subtle effect created by the similarity of these two structures.

3. Continuation of resistance in *Anne of Cleves*

We come now to the third and final stage of the main history in *Anne of Cleves*: The left shape in Fig 3.19 shows the deepened bay, for example, as it occurs in the veil described above. Most crucially, observe that the two arrows shown in this shape are the two resistance processes we discussed. Stage 3 of the history is this: These two resistance processes continue till they push into the bay as shown in the right shape of Fig 3.19. What has happened is that *each* of the two arrows has undergone the Second Evolution Law of the Process-Grammar, as follows:

First consider the left arrow on the left shape. Isolate it as shown in the left curve in Fig 3.20. It is, of course, a resistance arrow, terminating at a M^- extremum. Now, in the transition being described, this arrow has continued, till it pushed the curve inwards, as shown in the right curve in Fig 3.20.

What has happened in terms of the extrema involved is this: The M^- in the left curve has changed into the M^+ in the right curve. Furthermore, on either side of the M^+ extremum, there is now a dot. As noted before, a dot marks a place where the curvature

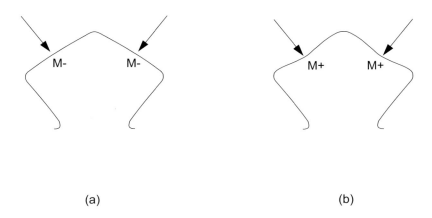

(a)   (b)

Figure 3.19: Continuation at the M^-.

is zero (flat). Such a point always occurs where the curve fluctuates from going inward to going outward (or vice versa).

The situation in the right curve in Fig 3.20 can of course be represented as a *triple* of crucial points: the central M^+ extremum together with the two points of zero curvature, 0, on either side. This triple is simply $0M^+0$.

Therefore the transition from the left curve to the right curve in Fig 3.20 can be described by saying that the M^- in the left curve has been replaced by the triple, $0M^+0$, in the right curve:

$$M^- \longrightarrow 0M^+0.$$

This is the Second Evolution Law of the Process-Grammar. This law is *Continuation of resistance* (CM^-). Observe that the *compressive* extremum in the left curve, has changed into the *penetrative* extremum in the right curve.

Now return to the full diagram of the deepened bay, Fig 3.19. In the transition from the left shape to the right shape, the Second Evolution Law occurs on both the left and the right side of the bay. In order not to clutter the diagram, the dots have been omitted, but notice the fluctuating effect around the curve, due to having these zeros of curvature.

We now have the tools necessary to go back to the painting.

A subtle example of the above type of situation occurs at the top line of the head-wear, i.e., the highest line of the painting. The reader can inspect it in Fig 3.21. Observe that, on each side of the peak, there is a slight indentation.

Observe the difference between this line and the veil-line below it. The latter represents the previous stage in the process-history, that is, the left shape in Fig 3.19. On each side of the peak of the veil-line, there is a compressive extremum, as discussed previously. In contrast, on each side of the peak in the top line of the head-wear, there is a penetrative extremum. These two penetrative extrema are responsible for the undulating

(a)   (b)

Figure 3.20: Isolating the arrow in Continuation at the M^-.

effect along that top line.

The reader should note that this line, as it occurs in the painting, is, strictly speaking, the foreground-background reversal of the right shape in Fig 3.19. That is, the line surrounds positive space, the head-wear, and is itself surrounded by negative space, the background, which it overlaps. Thus the line is actually produced by the foreground-background reversal of the Second Evolution Law. This is the First Evolution Law, Continuation at m^+ (Cm^+).

Finally, notice that a similar structure occurs as the shoulder-line. We had previously described this as a simple shield – the arc shown in Fig 3.13b. However, this arc was an implied line, and in fact represents the past. Recall that this line was created by Stage 1 of the process-history, the bifurcation of protrusion, as shown by the branching arrows in Fig 3.13c. Now, the actual line in the painting is more developed than this. First, the neck really defines an upward protrusion – one that has, in fact, broken through, creating the head. This is, of course, Stage 2 in the three-stage history, which was described as a breaking-through. Finally, to either side of the neck there is an indentation of the shoulder-line. Each such indentation has been created in the manner that we have been describing – that is, each is an example of Stage 3 of the history, i.e., the continuation of a compressive extremum till it penetrates.

Thus the shoulder-line is produced successively by all three stages of the process-history.

Finally, again, to appreciate the unity of the painting, the reader should take time to look again at the drawing in Fig 3.21, and try to see the shoulder-line and the top line of the head-wear, simultaneously. In this way, one can experience the exquisite effect created by the similarly of these two structures.

Figure 3.21: Line drawing of painting.

3.15   The Entire History

We are now ready to put together the three-stage history that dominates the painting, and observe the sequential effect in terms of shape. The three stages are given by the following laws from the Process-Grammar (and their duals):

1. Bifurcation at m^- (Bm^-)**.**
2. Bifurcation at M^- (BM^-)**.**
3. Continuation at M^- (CM^-)**.**

The sequence of shapes produced by these stages are given in Fig 3.22. The starting shape (Fig 3.22a) is the bottom half of an ellipse. This also presents us with the crucial starting process – the downward penetrative arrow. The structure is exemplified by the bottom half of Anne's face and the necklaces below, that imitate it. Emotionally, they represent the downward plunge of her assertiveness.

(a)

(b)

(c)

(d)

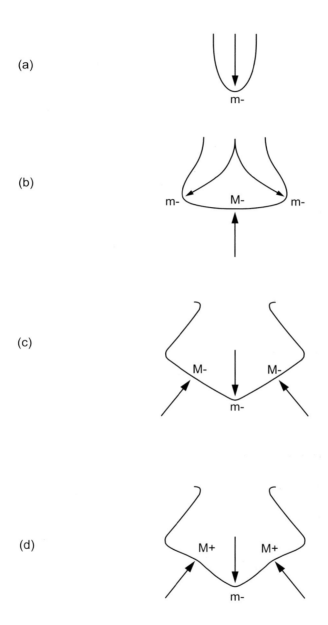

Figure 3.22: Entire history.

In the transition to Fig 3.22b, the process-arrow in the first shape, has met the upward oppositional force from the environment, and has therefore bifurcated. This second shape occurs in the dress-band, where the woman's defiance has branched to either side.

In the transition to Fig 3.22c, a new force appears from within her, at the center of the shape (m^-), and breaks down through the environmental opposition, thus reasserting her will. The environmental opposition is pushed to either side. The most prominent example of this structure appears as the downward vertex of the hands. Notice that, because the two M^- in Fig 3.22c are relics of the M^- in Fig 3.22b, one experiences a visual tension between the two forearm-lines and the dress-band. This illustrates my First Fundamental Law of Tension (p11) which states: Tension is the use of the Asymmetry Principle; i.e., it occurs from a present asymmetry to its past symmetry. The present asymmetry consists of the two side flat extrema of the deepened bay, and the past symmetry is the single central flat extremum of the ordinary bay. The tension goes between the two side extrema and the single extremum. The reader should carefully try to view this.

A quieter, more subtle, example of this structure is the line of the veil across her face.

In the final transition, to Fig 3.22d, the two side compressive forces have continued pushing till they penetrated, and the result is an undulation on either side of the central force. This structure is observable in the top of the head-wear, i.e., the top line of the painting, which is experienced as a subtle development of the veil-line just mentioned. However, the strongest example of this structure is the shoulder-line, with its upward force at the neck into the head, and an undulation on either side of the neck. This undulation indicates a slight capitulation to the invasion of the external forces in her world.

The operations of the Process-Grammar reveal the stages of a psychological argument in the character of Anne of Cleves.

They show the argument to be an alternation between assertion, resistance, shielding, breaking-through, and invasion.

3.16   History on the Full Closed Shape

The history has been described with respect to one half of the closed shape, for example, starting with half of the ellipse, Fig 3.22a. However, additional understanding of the painting can now be gained if one considers the history as acting on a complete closed shape, as we shall now see.

The closed shape, from which the history starts, is the ellipse which is given by the woman's face. Pages 51-58 studied the process-structure of an ellipse – which is shown here again in Fig 3.23. There are two inward compressive forces and two outward penetrative forces. Therefore this starting shape already contains the expressive themes

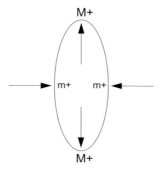

Figure 3.23: An ellipse has four extrema, and therefore four processes.

that will be exploited in the subsequent history – the inward compressive actions of society and outward assertion of self. It is worth the reader taking a moment to visualize the force-structure shown in Fig 3.23 directly onto the painting itself, Plate 6. The reader will be immediately surprised how strongly the force-structure conveys crucial aspects of the emotional expressiveness of the face.

Now, the arrows on the ellipse, Fig 3.23, represent a set of actions that produced the ellipse from a prior shape. The consequence of this is that there was a historical phase before to the ellipse, and this stage precedes the three stages presented above! That is, the total history is actually a four-stage history.

One recovers the initial state by simply undoing the effects of the arrows on the ellipse, i.e., pulling the ellipse back along the arrows. As said in the previous chapter, this leads back to a circle – the shape without curvature extrema.

In fact, the circle actually appears in the painting: around the head of the woman, as shown in Fig 3.24. This is the boundary line of the band of braid that surrounds her face, as can be seen in the painting itself, Plate 6. A circular arc also appears strongly as the neck-band.

A circle is the most symmetrical shape possible, and the Symmetry Principle (p7) states that a symmetry is understood as having always existed. The principle therefore implies that the circular shape around the woman's face carries a sense of *eternity*. And indeed this is emotionally what one feels from this shape.

We conclude that the history starts with the circle, and consists of the following four stages: The first is the conversion of the circle into the ellipse. The next three are those described above.

Additional insights into the painting will now be obtained by considering this four-stage history, as follows:

In the first stage, the introduction of the curvature extrema (producing the ellipse) takes place via the *bifurcation operations*. Thus, for example, the introduction of the penetrative extremum, at the bottom of the ellipse, is produced by a breaking-through, which is an occurrence of the Fifth or Sixth Evolution Law, depending on whether the interior of the ellipse is regarded as positive or negative space.

Figure 3.24: The presence of the circle.

When this breaking-through occurs in the painting, we shall call it the *first breaking-through*, because there will be another one later in the history. Clearly, the bottom of the chin is an example of the first breaking-through.

In the second historical stage, the two penetrative extrema on the ellipse each bifurcate to produce a bay. Thus the penetrative extremum at the bottom of the ellipse descends through the sequence of necklaces, to bifurcate into the bay in the dress-band; and the penetrative extremum at the top of the ellipse bifurcates to become the bay of the veil.

The consequence is that the ellipse has changed into the shape shown in Fig 3.25a, which we will call the *double-bay*. As will be seen, there are a number of reasons why it is valuable to understand the two bays as part of a single cohesive shape. One reason is that two additional extrema become apparent. These are the two side extrema that form the neck in Fig 3.25a. The neck is as important a part of the painting as anything discussed so far. Let us fully understand its role, as follows:

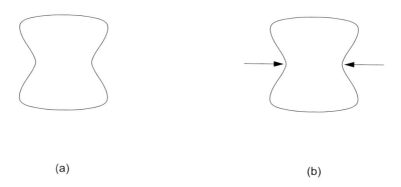

(a) (b)

Figure 3.25: Double-bay.

The neck consists of two inward penetrative extrema, caused by the two process-arrows in Fig 3.25b.

In fact it is important to see where these two arrows originate: The previous historical stage was the ellipse with the process-structure shown in Fig 3.23. One can see that what has happened, in the transition from the ellipse in Fig 3.23 to the shape in Fig 3.25b, is that the two compressive sideways arrows on the ellipse have continued till they penetrated. We shall call this, *the first continuation*, because there will be another continuation later in the history.

The first continuation is given by either the First or the Second Evolution Law, depending on one's assignment of positive and negative space. For ease of exposition, we will – for the entire remainder of this section – describe the shape as enclosing negative space, since we refer to the top and bottom as a bay. (As seen above, the shape occurs both as a bay, and its figure-ground reversal, a shield.) With this assumption, the law that creates the neck from the processes on the sides of the ellipse is the Second Evolution Law.

The historical change from the compressive arrows, on the sides of the ellipse in Fig 3.23, to the penetrative arrows on the sides of the neck in Fig 3.25b, is crucial to the painting. Thus let us look at the painting itself. Consider the ellipse formed by the face. Contrast this with the cohesive double-bay where the top and bottom bay are the veil and dress-band – and the neck is the woman's actual neck. What the reader should observe is the tension that exists between the outwardly-arched, yet compressed, sides of the face, and the inward penetrative sides of the neck. As shown in the previous paragraph, the tension is exactly described by the Second Evolution Law.

Having considered the process-structure of the neck in Fig 3.25b. Let us now consider the entire process-structure of this shape. This is shown in Fig 3.26b. Besides the two arrows of the neck, there are the three arrows of the bay at the top, and the three arrows of the bay at the bottom. Each set of three consists of two bifurcating arrows and a central vertical resistance arrow.

This entire set of eight arrows must have arisen historically from the arrows of the ellipse, as follows:

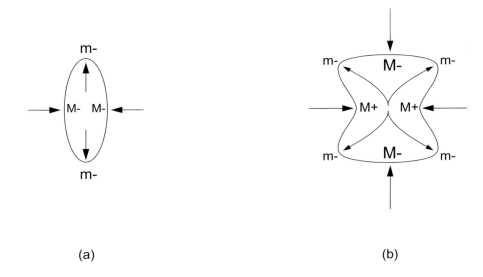

(a)   (b)

Figure 3.26: Evolution of the double-bay.

(1) The three arrows of the top bay in Fig 3.26b came from the single arrow at the top of the ellipse in Fig 3.26a. The law that determined the transition here was obviously bay-formation, i.e., *Bifurcation at* $m^-(Bm^-)$.

(2) The same Evolution Law was used for the bottom bay in Fig 3.26b.

(3) The arrow on the left side of the neck in Fig 3.26b, came from the inward arrow on the left of the ellipse in Fig 3.26a. The law that determined the transition here was the Second Evolution Law, i.e., *Continuation at* M^- (CM^-).

(4) The same Evolution Law was used for the arrow on the right side of the neck in Fig 3.26b.

This leads to the following crucial conclusion: Each of the four arrows on the ellipse is assigned its own Evolution Law from the Process-Grammar.

The above example illustrates the fact that the Evolution Laws are distributed at the extrema around the shape, and describe the different evolutionary changes that occur at the extrema. Each of the laws captures a different type of tension, and the arrangement of the laws around the shape captures the arrangement of the different types of tension on the shape.

We have just completed the first two stages in the four-stage history used in the painting. In the first stage, the circle changes to an ellipse. In the second stage, the ellipse changes into the double-bay. The final two stages each involve a modification of

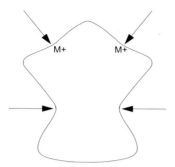

Figure 3.27: Evolution of the double-bay.

the bays on the shape.

Thus the third historical stage is a breaking-through at the center of each bay. For example, as seen earlier, the center of the bottom bay breaks through to become the vertex at the hands. And similarly, the top bay breaks through to become the upward vertex in the veil.

These are examples of what will be called the *second* breaking-through. The first was that which occurred in the transition of the circle to the ellipse, i.e., the introduction of the penetrative extrema at the bottom and top of the ellipse. The second is that which occurs at the center of the bay and produces what we call the deepened bay.

Although the first and second breaking-through occur on two different shapes – the circle and the double-bay respectively – they are produced by the same evolution laws. Thus, one visually experiences the breaking-through at the chin, and the breaking-through at the hands, as similar to each other. The reader should take a moment to view this beautiful similarity in the work.

In the final stage of the history, the compressive extrema, on either side of the center of the deepened bay, continue till they penetrate. For example, this effect is shown at the top of Fig 3.27. We saw this structure in the top line of the painting, and also in the shoulder.

The four-stage history can now be stated, as it applies to the *closed shape*. The history begins with a circle, and then the following four changes are successively applied:

1. **First breaking-through (BM^-).**
2. **First continuation (CM^-), and bay-formation (Bm^-).**
3. **Second breaking-through (BM^-).**
4. **Second continuation (CM^-).**

The history demonstrates a crucial type of unity that exists in a great painting, which our method of analysis has been able to reveal: The same Evolution Laws can be repeated at different stages of the history. Thus, we have seen that the breaking-through

Figure 3.28: Gauguin, *Vision after the Sermon*.

law, BM^-, is used twice at different stages; and this is interleaved with the continuation law, CM^-, which is also used twice at different stages. The effect of this unification is visually very powerful because, at each stage, a different shape has emerged – and yet the shape can receive an action at one of its points that recalls an action that occurred at an earlier stage.

3.17   Gauguin: *Vision after the Sermon*

To complete this chapter, we will look briefly at two more paintings. The first is Gauguin's *Vision after the Sermon*, also called *Jacob Wrestling with the Angel*. This is shown as Plate 7. Some basic aspects of its composition will now be discussed.

   The work comes from one of Gauguin's periods in Brittany, where he and a group of artists had escaped Paris to reclaim primitivism and its ethical power, which the artists saw in the local inhabitants, with their hardship and their spiritual concentration. These Breton women are returning from a plain Sunday morning in the white stone light of a

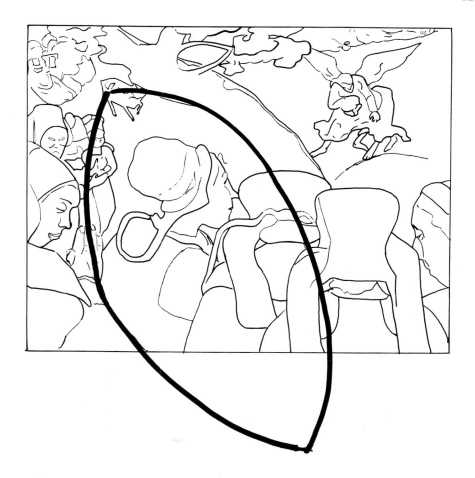

Figure 3.29: Largest shape of the painting.

cold church, and pass a field in which the very subject of the sermon – Jacob wrestling the angel – is awakened in the sunlit soil of their home.

Gauguin is here influenced by his companion, the artist Emil Bernard, who was the first to translate the rigid power of these peasants into the values of modern art – the granite flatness, the sense of existential assertion that can come from the arrangement of tension in the work.

To study the painting, we will use the line-drawing in Fig 3.28 which exhibits the shape-structure very clearly. It rests on strong compressive extrema, as follows:

The largest shape of the painting is the implied one shown in Fig 3.29. By comparing this figure with Fig 3.28, without the bold line, one can see exactly how Gauguin sets up the shape: One of its sides is the curved tree-trunk that cuts across the upper half of the painting. Its other side is the curve which is defined by the upward-pointing praying

Figure 3.30: The compressive forces on an ellipse.

hands of the woman on the lower left. Notice from Fig 3.28, how the latter curve starts at the bottom edge of the painting, with the line of her arm, then follows the hands into the edge of the clustered group of women, until it hits the cow at its peak by the tree. These two curved lines are sufficiently strong to imply that they run off the edge of the painting, below the work, and meet. Thus they imply a complete closed shape, as shown Fig 3.29.

The rules for the extraction of history from curvature extrema infer that the two sides of this shape have the two forces shown in Fig 3.30. Furthermore, the flattened extrema that constitute the sides of the shape are repeated at the tops of the bonnets and shoulders of the women. Considering the communicative content of these extrema, we observe that the emotional characteristics are indeed the six historical characteristics listed earlier for this extremum type (m^+), that is: *compressive, flattening, broadening, oppositional, inward, squashing.* These are directly inferred from the geometry by our rules, yet they clearly convey the psychological state of the women.

Notice also that the shapes of the bonnets recall the shape of the head-wear in the *Anne of Cleves.* However, there is a crucial difference. Gauguin does not add the further historical stages to these shapes, i.e., the central upward breaking-through and subsequent undulation. These bonnets remain flattened, remain compressed. The result is that the emotional expression is very different: Here the women convey a much greater sense of oppression; i.e., there is no upward breaking-through of liberation. That is, the tops of their heads are purely *compressed*, and therefore have the structure of what I call a *shield* – which represents the numbed, beaten-down, condition of their lives.

3.18   Memling: *Portrait of a Man*

Let us now consider Hans Memling's *Portrait of a Man*, shown in Plate 8. The face communicates considerable psychological strength and resilience. This is achieved through a pervasive use of the curvature rules given in this book, as follows:

Recall, in our study of *Anne of Cleves*, what was said about the structure of the hands. The downward vertex, shown in Fig 3.16, page 109, is created by a breaking-through operation. The visual implication is that, prior to the breaking-through, the hands had a similar structure to the bottom of the dress-band – with an upward compressive force

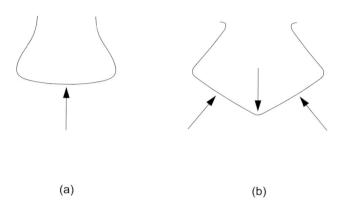

Figure 3.31: Bifurcation at M^-.

against a flat extremum at the center. However, the assertiveness of the woman countered this compressive action, by a downward penetrative force that created the vertex at the hands, and split the upward compressive force into two copies that were pushed to either side, so that they are now acting upward against the two forearms. The operation is shown again, in Fig 3.31 in the transition from the central compressive arrow in the left shape, to the triple of arrows into which it bifurcates in the right shape.

Memling, in his *Portrait of a Man*, entirely constructs the face from the repeated use of this single operation, as follows: First consider the left edge of the face (left with respect to the viewer). As shown in Fig 3.32, the cheekbone is the outward breaking-through of a penetrative force, and on either side of this extremum there are the two inward compressive forces.

One can think of the face as initially circular, and the operation just described as occurring at a set of points around the face, so as to give the face a hexagonal structure. Going clockwise, the six vertexes are at the cheekbone, the left corner in the hairline, the right corner of the hairline, the ear, the right end of the jaw, and the left end of the chin.

So fundamental is the breaking-through operation to the psychological feeling which Memling is trying to convey that the artist ensures that it is used to construct virtually every structure in the face. For example, consider the line that surrounds the right eye (right with respect to the viewer). The line is shown in Fig 3.33. Observe the breaking-through that occurs at the top center of the eyebrow. It has exactly the structure we described at the cheekbone. In fact, the entire line, starting with the shadow-line of the nose, and continuing through the eyebrow to its end – is created by the repeated use of this operation.

Exactly the same device is used to create the corresponding line around the other eye. As can be seen in Fig 3.33, this latter line consists of the left edge of the nose and continues as the eyebrow.

Figure 3.32: Left edge of the face.

Figure 3.33: Eye-brow lines.

The structure is repeated throughout the entire painting. For example, the shadows on the right side of the face (viewer's right) are built up in successive glazes – layers of shadows upon shadows – the edges of each having the structure just described. Furthermore, it is repeated in the clothing below. For example, the top half of the hexagonal face constituting the hair-line, is imitated below as the line of the collar against the man's neck.

3.19   Tension and Expression

One of the primary statements of Chapter 1 was this:

TENSION   ≡   MEMORY STORAGE.

Furthermore, one of the primary statements of Chapter 2 was this:

EMOTIONAL EXPRESSION   ≡   MEMORY STORAGE.

Thus, according to the theory being proposed in this book, both tension and emotional expression are equivalent to memory storage. Given this, I will now propose the relationship between tension and emotional expression:

**FUNDAMENTAL RELATION BETWEEN
TENSION AND EMOTIONAL EXPRESSION**

Tension views the stored process-history in the backward-time direction.

Emotional expression views the stored process-history in the forward time direction.

To understand this, consider the following: First recall that the First Fundamental Law of Tension (p11) states that tension is the use of the Asymmetry Principle: That is, tension goes from the present asymmetry to the past symmetry. Tension is the force in the present distorted state, that tries to make the shape return to its past undistorted version. This means that tension is directed backwards in time.

In contrast, expression goes in the reverse direction – from the past to the present. It is the force that acted on the past undistorted state, and changed it into the present distorted one. For example, to create an expression in the face, the person distorts the face with a force. Because this force was applied to the past undistorted face to obtain the present distorted one, it goes in the forward time direction.

Notice that the tension in the distorted face, seeks to return it to the previous non-distorted version. As we said, tension is directed in the backwards time direction. Thus, to restate: *Tension and expression act in the opposite directions of time.*

The consequence in terms of diagrams should be understood: We have had a number of figures with arrows on them representing the forward direction of time. This means that they represent the force of expression. To obtain the corresponding force of tension, one merely takes the arrows and reverses them.

Throughout this book, to avoid confusion, the arrows on shapes consistently represent the forward direction of time. Thus the diagrams always represent expressive forces. However, these figures will be referred to equally as expressive or tension structures. This will not create confusion. Again, to obtain the tension diagrams, one simply has to reverse the arrows.

Finally, the crucial point to emphasize is this: Both tension and emotional expression correspond to the *recovered* process-history. Tension views the recovered history in the backward time direction (present to past); and emotional expression views the same history in the forward time direction (past to present). Both therefore correspond to the *stored* process-history; i.e., the memory storage.

Chapter 4

Smoothness-Breaking

4.1 Introduction

We come now to another crucial factor in the extraction of process-history from curvature extrema. It concerns the breaking of smoothness. At the top of the curve in Fig 4.1b, there is a non-smooth extremum. This contrasts with the smooth extremum at the top of Fig 4.1a. Clearly, the point at the top Fig 4.1b has a particular quality of sharpness that the rest of the points on that curve, and all of the points on Fig 4.1a, do not possess.

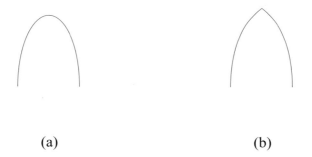

(a)   (b)

Figure 4.1: (a) A smooth extremum. (b) A non-smooth extremum.

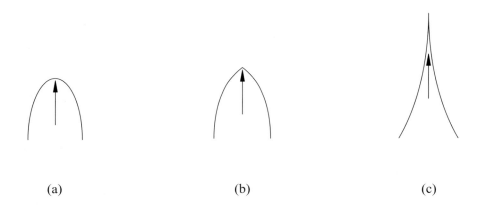

(a)   (b)   (c)

Figure 4.2: The three-stage scenario.

The effect of a non-smooth extremum is visually significant in a painting. There is a very visible sense of excitement that accumulates at such a point. It is necessary to completely explain this, in order to carry out analyses of paintings, for example, by Picasso, Balthus, Ingres, and Modigliani, which we shall do immediately after developing a theory of non-smoothness.

Non-smoothness involves an extra *historical* stage – a stage that breaks smoothness. This is inferred, once again, by the Asymmetry Principle. The reason is that a non-smooth point involves an extra asymmetry not possessed by smooth points.

The issues that arise in the breaking of smoothness are captured by the three-stage scenario shown in Fig 4.2. These stages can be described in the following way: Imagine that a knife is pushing on a curve made of rubber. The point of the knife will create a curvature extremum, shown at the top of Fig 4.2a. Initially, this extremum will be smooth because there is always some stiffness in a physical curve, no matter how flexible it is. Engineers refer to this as *flexural rigidity*. However, if the amount of force applied by the knife is increased, then it can eventually overcome the flexural rigidity, and a sharp crease will appear in the curve, as shown in Fig 4.2b. This will be called a *corner*. A still further stage can also occur. If the knife continues to push deeper, eventually a *cusp* can be formed as shown in Fig 4.2c. The entire Fig 4.2 therefore shows a three-stage scenario:

smooth extremum $\longrightarrow$ corner $\longrightarrow$ cusp.

The above scenario was invented in joint research I did with Pat Hayes (see Hayes & Leyton, [3]; Leyton & Hayes, [20]). Over the next two sections, we will recapitulate some of that research. What will be added here, however, is the involvement of the Asymmetry Principle. We will then be able to return to the structure of paintings.

4.2 The Smoothness-Breaking Operation

The first issue to be dealt with is *corners*. While, in the analyses of paintings in the previous chapters, an attempt was made to confine the discussion to smooth extrema, it was almost inevitable that examples of non-smooth extrema also occurred in the paintings, and these were handled in the same way as smooth extrema. This strategy was in fact appropriate in the following sense: The rules for smooth extrema also apply to non-smooth extrema. However, non-smooth extrema involve an additional rule. It is necessary to fully understand how this rule arises, as follows:

A curvature extremum is an asymmetry because it is a violation in the (rotational) symmetry of a circle, i.e., whereas a circle has equal curvature (bend) at each of its points, a curvature extremum necessarily involves differences in curvature along the curve.

However, despite this, a curvature extremum such as Fig 4.1a retains a particular symmetry possessed by the circle: A circle is smooth all around it. Similarly, Fig 4.1a is smooth all along it. Thus, with respect to the property of smoothness, the extremum at the top of Fig 4.1a is indistinguishable from the remainder of that curve. We can therefore say this:

> While a smooth extremum introduces distinguishability (asymmetry) with respect to curvature, it nevertheless retains indistinguishability (symmetry) with respect to smoothness.

Now contrast this with the case of the corner shown in Fig 4.1b. Here, smoothness exists everywhere along the curve except at one place, the extremum at the top. Thus, in this case, the extremum is a distinguishability with respect to the property of smoothness. The consequence is this:

> A non-smooth extremum has two asymmetries. It has distinguishability in curvature, just like a smooth extremum. However, it has an additional distinguishability: violation in smoothness.

It was noted earlier that there appears to be an extra level of visual excitement at a non-smooth extremum. The claim being made here is that this is due to the extra asymmetry that occurs at such an extremum.

Now, to define this asymmetry more fully, we have the following:

> *The curvature at a corner is infinite.*

Let us see why. The discussion in the next two paragraphs will be non-technical for readers without a background in differential geometry. At any point P on a smooth planar curve, the *curvature* is the *amount of bend*. What is called the *circle of curvature* at P is the circle that best approximates the curve at P, in the sense that it has the same curvature as the curve at P, shares the same tangent, and lies on the side toward which the curve is bending. Clearly, as can be seen in Fig 4.3a, at an smooth curvature extremum, one can find such a circle, because the curvature is finite at the extremum.

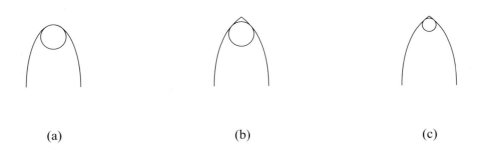

(a)   (b)   (c)

Figure 4.3: A finite circle reaches a smooth extremum but not a non-smooth one.

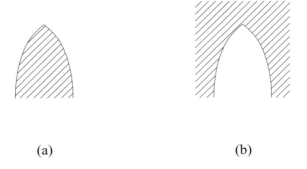

(a)   (b)

Figure 4.4: Positive vs. negative space.

Now let us consider the curve in Fig 4.3b, which has a corner at the top. A circle has been fitted into the curve. However, it does not touch the extremum. For it to do so, it has to reach further upwards, and this means that it has to be made smaller. However, no matter how small it becomes, if it still remains finite, then there would always be a gap between the circle and the corner, as can be seen in Fig 4.3c. The only way the circle could finally touch the corner, would be if the circle were made infinitely small.

Observe now that the smaller a circle is, the greater is its bend, e.g., a car would have to be turned more, in order to drive around the circle. Therefore, an infinitely small circle must have infinite bend. Thus, since only an infinitely small circle can reach the sharp extremum, this extremum must have infinite curvature.

The next thing to be understood is this:

> *The curvature at a corner, although infinite, can be positive infinite or negative infinite.*

The reason is as follows: Recall that, if a shape bends out, its curvature is positive; and if the shape bends in, the curvature is negative. Thus, the curvature of a protrusion is positive, and the curvature of an indentation is negative.

Fig 4.4a shows a curve with a corner at the top. The shading indicates the solid side of the curve; and the absence of shading indicates the empty side. Clearly the curve bends out at the top. Therefore it has positive curvature. Thus, although the corner point has infinite curvature, this infinity is positive.

In contrast, Fig 4.4b shows the same curve but with solid and empty space reversed. In this case, the curve bends into the solid, at the top. Therefore it has negative curvature. Thus, although the corner point has infinite curvature, this infinity is negative.

It is possible to proceed now to understand what happens when one sees a non-smooth extremum in a painting such as Picasso's *Demoiselles d'Avignon*, which will soon be examined. First, we must use the Asymmetry Principle, which says that an asymmetry in the present must go back to a symmetry in the past. Thus, given a non-smooth extremum such as that in Fig 4.5, the principle says that the infinite curvature that distinguishes the top point from all the other points on the curve, must be removed backwards in time. That is, as one goes into the past, the infinite curvature must become finite; i.e., the top point must be smoothed out.

Figure 4.5: A non-smooth extremum.

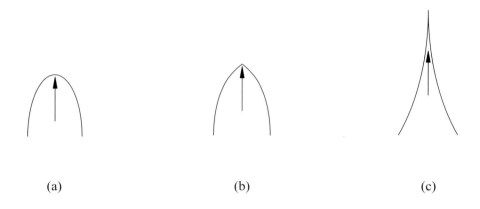

(a)   (b)   (c)

Figure 4.6: The three-stage scenario.

This implies that, forwards in time, there was a breaking of smoothness. Following the research of Hayes and Leyton, this transition will be represented in the following way:

$$\kappa : e \longrightarrow e_\kappa$$

From left to right, this reads as follows: Smoothness-breaking κ takes an extremum e, of finite curvature, and replaces it by the extremum e_κ, of infinite curvature, which is the same type (Max or min) as the original extremum.

4.3 Cusp-Formation

Let us now return to the three-stage scenario shown again in Fig 4.6. In the first stage, there is the production of the smooth extremum Fig 4.6a from a circle. This was dealt with in our initial rules for the extraction of process-history from curvature extrema. In the second stage, there is the breaking of smoothness resulting in Fig 4.6b. This has been dealt with in the last section. We now come onto the final stage, the production of the cusp, shown in Fig 4.6c.

How does the cusp differ from the ordinary corner shown in Fig 4.6b? The answer is given in Fig 4.7, as follows: Let us assume, for a moment that the solid part of the shape is within the curve. Then one can see that the shape in Fig 4.7a bends outward all the way around it, as indicated by the three plus signs. This contrasts with the cusp in Fig 4.7b, which is more subtle: Here, as indicated by the negative signs, the curve bends inward at the two sides. However, at the top point, the curve still bends outwards.

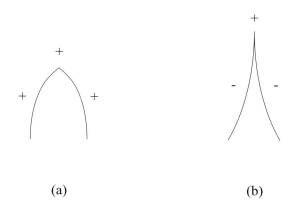

Figure 4.7: Distribution of positive and negative curvature.

The analogous structure exists where the inside of the curve is empty and the outside is solid. In this case, the corner would have a negative sign all the way around, and the cusp would have positive signs on the two sides with a negative sign at the top. Thus generally we conclude:

> *At a corner, the sign of the curvature on either side of the extremum is the same as at the extremum point itself. At a cusp, the sign of the curvature on either side of the extremum is the opposite from that at the extremum point.*

Having understood what a cusp is structurally, let us now consider the inference of its history. Suppose one is presented with a cusp in a painting. How does one infer its past? In fact, how does one infer that the past of Fig 4.6c was the corner in Fig 4.6b. Of course, once one has recovered the corner, one can infer the past of *that* by using the smoothness-breaking rule of the last section. However, it is necessary to have a rule to get us from the cusp back to the corner.

The answer is given, once more, by my First Fundamental Law of Memory Storage, the Asymmetry Principle, which says that an asymmetry in the present is understood as having arisen from a past symmetry. To apply this here, consider the cusp in Fig 4.7b. The asymmetry that exists is the difference in sign between the sides and the extremum itself. According to the Asymmetry Principle, this difference has to be removed backward in time; the signs have to be made equal. This recovers the corner shown in Fig 4.7a.

Finally, let us consider the following issue. In going forwards in time, the transition from the smooth extremum in Fig 4.6a, to the corner in Fig 4.6b, was given by the smoothness-breaking operation κ. This operation was a rule that had to be added to the system of curvature rules given previously. The question to ask now is this: What operation gives the transition from the corner in Fig 4.6b to the cusp in Fig 4.6c; that is, produces the sign-asymmetry of the cusp from the sign-symmetry of the corner?

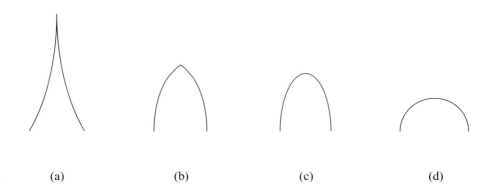

(a)   (b)   (c)   (d)

Figure 4.8: Recovered history from a cusp.

It turns out that a new operation is not required in addition to the set of operations so far provided. The six evolution laws, constituting the Process-Grammar, will create this asymmetry.

4.4   Always the Asymmetry Principle

The following fundamental fact should now be observed: In the entire backward history, it is the Asymmetry Principle that is used, at each stage, to go back to the preceding stage. This fact is so important that it must be examined carefully, as follows:

Suppose that the present contains a cusp, for example, that shown in Fig 4.8a. Let us see how the entire history of the cusp is recovered. In order to emphasize the point to be made, we will assume that the present contains no other shape but the cusp; i.e., no other *records* of the past history. Thus, all historical information must be *inferred*; and it must be inferred from the only data available in the present, the cusp itself. The successive stages, backwards in time, are recovered in the following way:

(1) On the cusp, the sides have a different sign from the extremum point. In accord with the Asymmetry Principle, this difference has to be removed backwards in time. As a result, one obtains the corner, shown in Fig 4.8b.

(2) On the corner, the sides have finite curvature, whereas the extremum point itself

has infinite curvature. In accord with the Asymmetry Principle, this difference must be removed backwards in time. As a result, one obtains the smooth extremum, shown in Fig 4.8c.

(3) On the smooth extremum, the curvature is different at the different points around the curve. In accord with the Asymmetry Principle, this difference in curvatures must be removed backwards in time. As a result, one obtains the only shape in which there is no difference in curvature around the curve: the circle – as shown in Fig 4.8d.

The sequence of diagrams, Fig 4.8a, b, c, d therefore show the entire recovered history backwards in time. What we have seen is that, at each stage, one uses the Asymmetry Principle to obtain the preceding stage.

4.5 Cusp-Formation in Compressive Extrema

In the above discussion of smoothness-breaking, several diagrams were drawn to illustrate the argument. However, the attentive reader will have observed that, in each diagram, the smooth extremum that was drawn was penetrative. In fact, the scenario we have just been discussing applies to penetrative extrema. Although the scenario for compressive extrema involves exactly the same asymmetries, the results are different. It will soon be seen that this difference has been exploited by artists such as Picasso.

Fig 4.9a shows a compressive extremum, with the usual downward force creating the flattening effect. Let us now suppose that this force is sharp enough to actually break the smoothness. The result is shown in Fig 4.9b. It has the usual asymmetry of broken-smoothness: The curve on either side of the extremum point has finite curvature, in contrast to the extremum point itself which has infinite curvature.

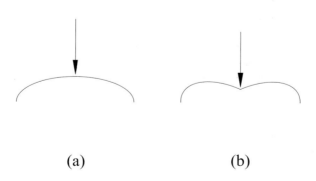

(a)   (b)

Figure 4.9: A compressive force that is sharp.

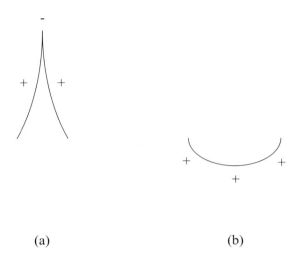

(a)   (b)

Figure 4.10: Distribution of positive and negative curvatures.

However, observe that this shape also contains the asymmetry that defines the cusp: That is, the sign of the curve on either side of the extremum point is the opposite of the sign of the point itself. The reason is that, whereas the curve on either side bends out from the enclosed shape, the curve at the extremum point bends into it.

One sees therefore that, while the transition from the left shape to the right shape in Fig 4.9 is created by the smoothness-breaking operation, this operation introduces not only the usual asymmetry of broken-smoothness, but also the asymmetry defining a cusp.

The conclusion is therefore this: For compressive extrema, smoothness-breaking and cusp-formation are forced to occur simultaneously. There is in fact a rigorous mathematical reason why this necessarily has to take place – which is elaborated in the research of Hayes and Leyton. Rather than presenting that argument here, an alternative reason will now be given using the Asymmetry Principle.

Let us consider the cusp shown in Fig 4.10a. For the sake of argument, assume that the empty space is on the inside, and that therefore the sides have positive curvature, with the extremum point having negative curvature.

Now let us use the Asymmetry Principle on this asymmetry. As noted before, this principle implies that, backwards in time, the signs become the same. However, observe now that there are two alternative ways that this can happen:

(1) The signs at the sides can change to become the same as the sign at the top. This is what happened in the previous section. It lead to a penetrative extremum, backward in time.

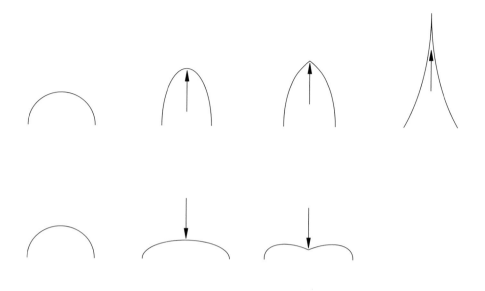

Figure 4.11: The two histories.

(2) Alternatively, the sign at the top can change to become the same as the sign at the sides. In this case, we get the situation shown in Fig 4.10b. That is, the extremum retracts and the result is the compressive extremum shown.

The cusp in the two alternative cases has exactly the same shape. We shall see that the factor that determines which of the two scenarios is chosen is the remainder of the curve on which the cusp occurs. Quite simply, one chooses to turn a cusp back into a penetrative extremum when the remainder of the curve stops one from turning it back into a compressive extremum. Similarly, one chooses to turn a cusp back into a compressive extremum when the remainder of the curve stops one from turning it back into a penetrative extremum. This will be illustrated shortly with paintings by Picasso.

It will now be seen that, despite the fact that the two cusps have the same shape, they have different expressive qualities. The reason is due to my Fundamental Law of Expression which states that emotional expression is recovered history.

Consider Fig 4.11, which shows the two histories involved. The upper sequence of shapes is the entire history for the penetrative case, and the lower sequence is the entire history for the compressive case. Both histories, of course, start with a circle. Notice how early, in each history, the characterizing extremum occurs: In the upper case, the penetrative extremum emerges in the *second* shape. Similarly, in the lower case, the compressive extremum also emerges in the second shape.

The most obvious difference between the histories concerns the relationship between the *force* and the *direction of the arch* on which it acts. In the upper case, the force goes in the direction of the arching; and in the lower case the force opposes the direction of the arching. In fact, what is being discussed here is the fourth historical characteristic of extrema. Recall that, with respect to this characteristic, a penetrative extremum is *facilitative* of the arching, and a compressive extremum is *oppositional* to the arching. The subsequent historical stages reflect this characteristic. Thus, in the upper case, the history has an elongating effect on the arch, whereas, in the lower case, the process continues to oppose the overall arch.

In accord with the Fundamental Law of Expression, these historical differences translate directly into the emotional differences between the two kinds of cusp. This will be seen in several examples later, but as an initial illustration, consider the two Picasso's shown in Fig 4.12a and 4.12b, as follows:

In Fig 4.12a, there is a downward cusp just above the woman's elbow. It forms the bottom part of the black area in Fig 4.12c – using the edge of the armchair and the downward edge of her shoulder. In the other painting, Fig 4.12b, there is a cusp forming the right side of the woman's upper breast – approximately where the stems of the flowers emerge.

Observe that the cusp in the left painting must have arisen from a penetrative extremum. In contrast, the cusp in the right painting arose from a compressive extremum: Picasso shows this by implying a connecting line above the cusp – given as a dotted line in Fig 4.12d. Notice that this line turns the body into an ellipse, and, as we know, the top extremum of an ellipse is a compressive extremum. The cusp here is seen as pushed down from the dotted line shown.

Now observe that the emotion expressed by the cusp in the left painting is very different from the emotion expressed by the cusp in the right painting. In the left painting, the cusp has the easy facilitative and elongated feeling, that was predicted above for cusps arising from penetrative extrema. In contrast, the cusp in the right painting has the tougher, more difficult, oppositional sense, that was predicted for cusps arising from compressive extrema. That is, the force seems to work against the flattened line above it. Rigorously: The two very different kinds of feeling correspond to the two very different inferred histories – in accord with our principle that emotional expression is recovered history.

4.6   The Bent Cusp

In the examples of paintings that will now be examined, there will sometimes occur the type of cusp illustrated in Fig 4.13b. This is a bent version of the ordinary cusp, and it contains an extra level of tension, because it has an extra asymmetry: One side bends *into* the symmetry axis, and the other side bends *out from* the axis. This was analyzed, in detail, in Chapter 6 of my book, *Symmetry, Causality, Mind*. In order not to assume knowledge of this other research, the present chapter will refer to bent cusps simply as "cusps".

Figure 4.12: Two Picasso's with their cusp-structures.

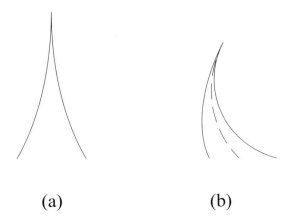

(a)   (b)

Figure 4.13: (a) Straight cusp. (b) Bent cusp.

4.7 **Picasso:** *Demoiselles d'Avignon*

A number of paintings will now be examined to illustrate the issues concerning smoothness. The first is Picasso's *Demoiselles d'Avignon*, shown as Plate 9. In this section, a
summary will be presented of the lengthy analysis I gave in *Symmetry, Causality, Mind*.

As said many times above, the ultimate starting shape with no curvature variation is
a circle. In fact, a circle is explicitly drawn by Picasso several times in the work. Fig
4.14 gives one of the examples. By comparing this diagram with the color photograph,
Plate 9, the reader will be able to see how clearly and firmly Picasso defines it. For
example, at point A, in Fig 4.14, the circle is the side of an arm; at point B it is the edge
of a shadow; at point C it is a line drawn on the back of the seated woman; and at point
D it is a black line in the drapery on the central woman.

Now the circle undergoes a succession of changes in the painting. First, it is stretched
into an ellipse. An example is shown in Fig 4.15. Observe again how Picasso explicitly
draws in this shape. For instance, by comparing Fig 4.15 with the color plate, one can
see that the lower left edge of the ellipse is clearly presented as the curved line across
the blue drapery.

Since an ellipse is obtained from a circle by stretching, one can say that an ellipse
embodies the following process theme:

1st PROCESS THEME: Stretching

As will be seen, stretching represents liberation in this painting. The use of the ellipse,
to convey this, is made repeatedly throughout the work.

Figure 4.14: One of the structuring circles.

The example in Fig 4.15 has a remarkably profound meaning: The cause of the stretching appears to be the *sight* by the upper right woman, as she looks in. Thus the liberating effect of stretching is created here by the act of seeing. The identification of liberation and seeing is crucially important in this painting, as will be observed later. In fact, we will show that the effect is that of *pulling the eye apart*.

In the next stage of the history, the ellipse is made pointed, as shown in Fig 4.16. This occurs as a result of applying the smoothness-breaking operation to each end. Recall that the breaking of smoothness means the overcoming of flexural rigidity. Thus we can say that the pointed ellipse introduces the second process theme in the painting:

2nd PROCESS THEME: Overcoming Rigidity

Pointed ellipses occur profusely throughout the painting, e.g., as many of the limbs of the women, as well as their hips, and their eyes and mouths. The breaking of smoothness gives a sense that the liberation is a violent one.

The next stage in the history of this shape is the breaking-through operation which was seen in Holbein's *Anne of Cleves* and Memling's *Portrait of a Man*. The operation is briefly recapitulated in the rest of this paragraph: Recall, for example, in our study of *Anne of Cleves*, that it creates the downward vertex at the hands, shown in Fig 3.16 (p109). The visual implication is that prior to the breaking-through, the hands had a similar structure to the bottom of the dress-band, which had an upward compressive force against a flat extremum at the center. However, in smoothness-breaking, the assertiveness of the

Figure 4.15: The resulting ellipse.

Figure 4.16: Pointed ellipse.

woman countered this compressive action, by a downward penetrative force that created the hand-vertex, and split the upward compressive force into two copies that were pushed to either side so that they are now acting against the two forearms. The operation is shown again in Fig 4.17 in the transition from the arrow in the left shape, to the three arrows on the right. Note that, depending on the assignment of foreground and background, the breaking-through operation is either the Fifth Evolution Law (Bifurcation of m^+) or the Sixth Evolution Law (Bifurcation of M^-).

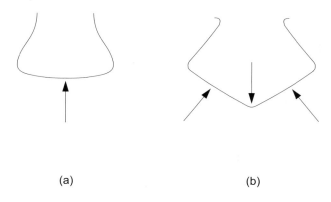

(a)   (b)

Figure 4.17: Breaking-through.

Now let us return to the *Demoiselles d'Avignon*. We had previously arrived at the stage of the pointed ellipse. The sides constitute compressive extrema, as shown for the left side in Fig 4.18a. What Picasso does at this stage is apply the breaking-through operation on both compressive extrema. Thus for example, Fig 4.18b shows the result on the left side. The inward compressive force has split into two copies that have been pushed apart under the outward action of the new penetrative force. The psychological meaning of the breaking-through is, of course, exactly the same as in the *Anne of Cleves* – and this reinforces my basic claim that emotional expression is the process-history inferred from the geometry.

The operation of breaking through is the third stage in the history used by Picasso, and I will therefore refer to it as the third process theme:

3rd PROCESS THEME: Breaking Through

In the next stage, the horizontal extrema in Fig 4.18b, themselves undergo the smoothness-breaking operation, κ, and this results in the diamond shown in Fig 4.19. Therefore, in this shape, one has the broken smoothness not only of the top and bottom extrema – which occurred previously at the ellipse stage – but also the left and right.

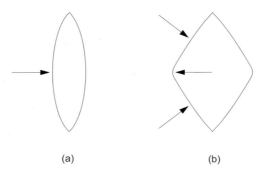

(a)   (b)

Figure 4.18: Breaking-through on the side of a pointed ellipse

The diamond is a very important shape in the painting. There are many examples of it, but none more significant than the diamond that constitutes the opening curtain in Fig 4.20. This is being pulled apart by the intruder on the upper right in order to view and enter the brothel. Thus one can state the fourth process theme to be this:

4th PROCESS THEME: Pulling Open

Observe how Picasso draws in the diamond on the canvas: By comparing Fig 4.20 with the color plate, we see that three of the sides are explicitly presented as physical lines – these are the top-left, top-right, and bottom-right sides. The remaining one, the bottom-left, is given as sequence of symmetry axes terminating at curvature extrema that lie along that line – for example, the powerful symmetry axis of the knee (of the woman in the bottom-right), as well as of the extrema lying further down the line towards the edge of the painting.

In the next stage of development, the sharp processes at the corners of the diamond, continue further and produce cusping, as in the transition from Fig 4.21a to Fig 4.21b.

It is worthwhile at this point considering the emotional quality of a cusp. Recall that, in the transition to a cusp, the curve on either side of the extremum undergoes a change in the sign of its curvature. The effect is that the curve pulls inwards towards the "knife" on the axis. Previously, the curve managed to resist this inward movement. But at the formation of the cusp, this resistance has been overcome.

Figure 4.19: The conversion to a diamond.

Figure 4.20: One of the main diamonds.

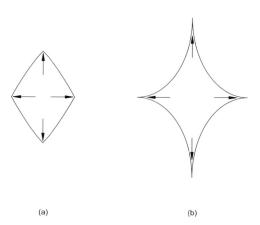

(a)   (b)

Figure 4.21: The corners of a diamond will continue, creating cusps.

Therefore, in the two successive stages, smoothness-breaking followed by cusp-formation, the knife successively conquers the curve, in the following way: At the smoothness-breaking stage, the knife overcomes the flexural rigidity at the extremum and produces the sharp point. At the subsequent cusp-formation stage, the curve collapses inwards toward the knife. We shall describe this collapsing as the final *yielding* of the curve to the knife. Therefore, cusp-formation introduces what I call the fifth process theme of the work:

5th PROCESS THEME: Yielding

The pulling-open theme also occurs in a different structural form, represented most prominently by the branching arms of the central woman, as shown in Fig 4.22. This structure is created by the bifurcation of a protrusion. The previous stage was the pointed ellipse, shown in Fig 4.16. The top extremum of the ellipse now undergoes bifurcation, producing the violent branching elbows of the woman. Notice that the bottom extremum of the ellipse is given by the vertex at the woman's pubic region.

The upward branching effect is a use of the Third Evolution Law, which is Bifurcation at M^+. Since this operation has not occurred in the previous stages of the painting, it will be identified as an additional historical theme in its own right:

6th PROCESS THEME: Branching Out

There is also a further historical factor involved in the branching: This is exemplified by the downward arrow at the top of Fig 4.22. Its effect is to counter the upward bifurcation of the protrusion with an indentation that tears apart the branching arrows. This is actually a use of the First Evolution Law, Cm^+. And again, since this operation has not occurred in the previous stages, it will be identified as an additional historical theme in its own right:

7th PROCESS THEME: Tearing Apart

It is important now for the reader to see that the arrows in the two arms are the ends of an upward process that extends over the entire height of the painting. This powerful movement starts with the curvature extremum of the table at the bottom of the painting, given by the lowest arrow in Fig 4.22. It is then continued by an upward arrow in the leg, given by the curvature extremum at the knee. Finally, the movement is caught by the upward branching from the woman's chest into her arms.

The crucial thing to observe, about the branching structure in Fig 4.22, is that its ultimate purpose is to tear the painting into two halves. Observe how this theme is echoed by other structures along the central vertical of the painting: First of all, as shown in Fig 4.23, the upward arrow leading to the knee actually continues and bifurcates into the hips. This structure echoes exactly the structure in the arms. Second, observe that the downward arrow in the belly, leading to the pubic region, continues and bifurcates into the legs of the women on either side – shown by the two downward arrows in Fig 4.23. Notice that the process that tears these latter two branches apart is the upward arrow of the knee.

Figure 4.22: Upward surge and branching out.

Figure 4.23: Central branchings.

4.8   The Meaning of *Demoiselles d'Avignon*

The meaning of *Demoiselles d'Avignon* will now be considered further. My Fundamental
Law of Expression states that emotional expression is recovered history. This history
is inferred from the shape structure of the painting using the laws of memory storage.
And, as I said in section 1.5, the meaning of an artwork is the process-history inferred
from its shape structure. Again this will be substantially illustrated here.

The previous section showed that there are seven historical actions that are recovered
from the shapes in this painting. Because they are used over and over again, I have called
them process themes. They are:

1st PROCESS THEME: Stretching.

2nd PROCESS THEME: Overcoming Rigidity.

3rd PROCESS THEME: Breaking Through.

4th PROCESS THEME: Pulling Open.

5th PROCESS THEME: Yielding.

6th PROCESS THEME: Branching Out.

7th PROCESS THEME: Tearing apart.

Let us consider the overall drama which these themes are used to serve. When one
examines these seven themes, one realizes that they have a common core: They are
the themes of revolution. That is, revolution is about *stretching, overcoming rigidity,
breaking-through, pulling open, yielding, branching out,* and *tearing apart.*

Picasso was of course strongly aware of the revolutionary character of the work in
relation to the preceding history of art. The painting is both a discussion of revolution
and an act of revolution.

But what is undergoing a revolution in this work? To answer this question, one must
remember that *Demoiselles d'Avignon* begins the cubist period, the most important single
movement in twentieth century art. Most of the major artistic developments of modern
art arise from analytic or synthetic cubism: complex multi-perspective, the dissolution
of three-dimensional form, the consequent abstraction, all-over composition, surface
flatness, differing levels of seeing, self-reference in seeing, the inclusion of literary
elements such as words, the democracy of materials, the assemblage of found objects,
etc. Not only are the discoveries of cubism pervasive throughout subsequent art, but they
are pervasive throughout all other media - film, video, newspaper cartoons, advertising,
etc.

What all these developments attest to is that cubism was first and foremost a *revolution in sight.* Indeed, so effective and total was this revolution in seeing that the media

which uses its discoveries – from film to advertising – are completely comprehensible to the general public, and indeed actively sought by the public.

Demoiselles d'Avignon, the first painting of the cubist period, begins the revolution in sight. Each of the seven process themes, elaborated above, concerns actions on shape – but the shape on which they operate represents sight. That is, going through the seven process themes, it is *sight* (1) which is *stretched*, (2) whose *rigidity is overcome*, (3) whose *resistance is broken through*, (4) which is *pulled open*, (5) which is *forced to yield*, (6) which *branches out*, (7) which is *torn apart*.

Now, as observed earlier, the ultimate past shape on which these actions operate is the circle, a significant shape of the painting. When one looks at the painting and discovers any one of the major circles, one has, at the moment of discovery, a sudden sensation of calmness, as one's eye expands to fill the circle. It is as if one's eye equates its own circular structure with the circle in the painting. This sensation is very strongly felt when looking at the actual painting in the Museum of Modern Art in New York, because, in the painting's massive size, the circles can have their full effect.

Thus, in acting on the circle, the various processes in the painting act on the circle of the eye. That is, when viewing the painting, one has the strong sensation that *one's eye is pulled apart*. This sensation, in the viewer's eye, matches the large-scale historical revolution in sight that was to be instituted by cubism.

The revolutionary action of the painting, while being central to its meaning for the viewer, as well as its meaning for modern art, was an intensely personal experience for Picasso himself. During this period, Picasso seems to have turned inward and become particularly concerned with his own creativity. That is, not only was he engrossed in the products of his creativity, but he was deeply pre-occupied with the creativity itself. Indeed, as I have argued many times: *The self-referential nature of the explanatory process defines the genius.*

Thus, while *Demoiselles d'Avignon* was the revolutionary outpouring of Picasso's creativity, so intense was this creativity that paradoxically, it became the subject of the painting. Creativity is again, the common core that runs through the seven process themes that define the history inferred from the painting's shapes. Of course, the way in which these themes embody revolutionary action is identical to the way in which they embody creativity. In life, there is often no distinction between revolutionary action and creativity.

Less obviously, we find that, in this painting, Picasso seems to have equated three concepts *sight*, *creativity*, and *sex*. Let us begin by considering the first two: In cubism, Picasso is the first artist to discover that sight is a creative act. Sight is an active exploration and manipulation of objects. Sight constructs the world, and in so doing, is a free agent.

Consider now the second two concepts: creativity and sex. It seems that, in this period of his life, while being so intensely focussed on the mystery of his own artistic fertility, Picasso identified it with the sexuality and fertility of women. This type of identification is not uncommon for an artist. For example, one sees it in the sketch-books of da Vinci, in the latter's obsessive studies of pregnancy.

The sexual content of *Demoiselles d'Avignon* is obvious. But why? Is it simply that the women are naked?

Recall our claim that the meaning of a painting is embodied in the history derived from its shape structure. Recall that we defined seven process themes in Picasso's painting: *stretching, overcoming rigidity, breaking-through, pulling open, yielding, branching out, tearing apart.* We have seen how these themes can be regarded as concerning both sight and the revolutionary aspects of creativity. But they can equally well be regarded as concerning the sexuality of women at the moment of intercourse and conception.

As an example, it is worth dwelling on the fourth process theme: the pulling-open theme. Since this theme is so central to the shape-structure of the painting, and since the painting has such a strong sexual content, it is difficult not to conclude that this process-theme embodies the parting of vaginal folds at the moment of sexual entrance into a woman. After all, the woman on the lower right of the painting sits with her legs wide open. Furthermore, her significance is undeniable. She is turning to face us. Her strong stare leads us into the painting.

Indeed, just as the image of her face has been presented to us only by the action of her turning, there is a way in which the whole painting is the image of her opening vagina which is hidden from us because her pelvis faces away from us, but which has been turned to face us in the entire structure of the painting. After all, the upper figure on the right is pulling open folds that encompass the full length of the painting. The large opening diamond-shape formed by these folds was shown in Fig 4.20. Once again, we see that the process-history inferred from the shape structure of the painting – the history of pulling open – embodies the meaning of the painting. That is, we see again that *the experience of the painting is the experience of extracting the stored memory.*

Now recall our noting that, in this period of his life, Picasso became deeply concerned with the mystery of his own creativity and that, furthermore, he identified his creativity with the sexuality of women.

This figure on the upper right, who opens an entrance into the scene, clearly embodies the sexual meaning of the painting. But, in so doing, it seems to be the case that, in this figure – who could be either male or female – Picasso is representing himself at this crucial moment of self-consciousness and artistic discovery. By painting this figure as staring into the sexual womb, Picasso identifies the act of sexual penetration with sight. Sight enters and fertilizes. Sight is the source of Picasso's creativity. The figure pulls apart the folds and the path that lies opened is the future of art. Picasso has equated sight, creativity, and sex. This triple identity is the *memory stored* in each shape of the painting. Each shape carries a role in each of three stories that Picasso makes one. And the story itself is elaborated in the shape structure of the painting. From the shapes, we recover the story – the history, that is the meaning of the painting. And the recovered history is Picasso's personal crisis and the crisis in modern art.

4.9   Balthus: *Thérèse*

We come now to two paintings from a series that Balthus made of Thérèse, in the late 1930's. They are shown as Plates 10 and 11.

Figure 4.24: Repetition of the face extremum.

When one first sees these works, one might be sufficiently offended by the unhealthy direction of their sexual focus, that one fails to notice that they are outstanding structural compositions. The first painting, *Thérèse*, will be analyzed in this section; and the other one, *Thérèse Dreaming*, will be examined in the next section.

Let us begin with the face in *Thérèse*. A face, as we have pointed out before, is a vertical ellipse, with downward and upward penetrative extremum at the bottom and top. Let us first consider how Balthus uses the bottom extremum.

Consider Fig 4.24. It shows that the bottom half of the face is copied as the downward plunging extremum in the center of the work. The latter extremum will be referred to as the central plunge of the painting.

We are going to analyze the role of the central plunge in great detail, but before doing so, some comments need to be made: The fact that the bottom half of the face is copied as the plunge, begins to show the power of Balthus as an artist. The general public think of a great portrait as one that achieves an exceptional life-like quality. This is not the case. What is important is that the structures of the face and limbs are used over and over again, as a vocabulary from which all the different parts of the canvas are created, so that the work forms an integrated whole based on those structures. One consequence of this unification is that, experientially, *the self becomes environment and the environment becomes self.* It will be argued, in a later volume, that this is central to the experience that a genius has in the world.

Most crucially, of course, Balthus takes the structures of the body, i.e., the positive space, and creates from them the structures of the background, i.e., the negative space. In Fig 4.24, the outline of the face encloses positive space – whereas the outline of the plunge encloses negative space (background). Thus, positive and negative space become integrated. The operation that goes from one to the other is, of course, the Duality Operator defined in section 2.7.

Before returning to a full analysis of the plunge, we must observe the powerful device by which Balthus sets it up: The crucial factor is the horizontal line that defines the top of the table in the background. Observe that this line continues leftward as the eyes, and thus establishes the eyes as a firm, grounded, factor in the composition. But observe also that the table-line is the line that is deformed downwards to become the plunge. Thus the table-line serves simultaneously two powerful structural roles – one with respect to the eyes, and the other with respect to the plunge. It thereby helps to enforce the crucial relationship between the face and the plunge.

Now we are ready to gain a deeper understanding of the plunge, as follows: We shall see that it occurs within a sequence of historical stages. The first, as just seen, is the table-line. The others are as follows:

The second occurs before reaching the central curve given in Fig 4.24: The initially straight line is bent slightly to become the arm-lines, shown in Fig 4.25a. Observe also that these two lines are quoted in an enlarged size as the pair of leg-lines in Fig 4.25b. This helps to establish the body itself as an integrated whole based on a single restricted set of structural motives.

The next stage of deformation is the plunge itself as given in Fig 4.24. This, of course, is a penetrative extremum. Subsequently, it undergoes two further stages in the painting – those defined in the discussion of smoothness-breaking: (1) the smoothness-breaking operation κ itself, in which a corner is formed, and (2) the subsequent formation of the cusp.

First consider the smoothness-breaking. This occurs in several places. However, perhaps the most significant is at the bottom of the painting, shown by the dark line in Fig 4.25c. This corner is formed by the chair. Balthus ensures two things: (1) The corner comes down to the bottom edge of the canvas; and (2) it is at the approximate center of the bottom edge. These two factors give a sense that the entire composition rests on the vertex.

The reader should observe that any sense that the composition might be unstable, because it is balanced on a pivot, is removed by two factors: (1) the girl's lower leg on the right, and (2) the chair-leg on the left – both of which reach the edge of the canvas. These two legs connect with a central pivot that is parallel to the bottom pivot, as shown in Fig 4.25d.

The symmetry of these two legs is crucial in establishing the strength of this structure. This is due to the Symmetry Principle (section 1.4), which states that any symmetry is understood as having always existed. It is therefore this principle that explains why the two legs contribute a sense of permanence to the composition.

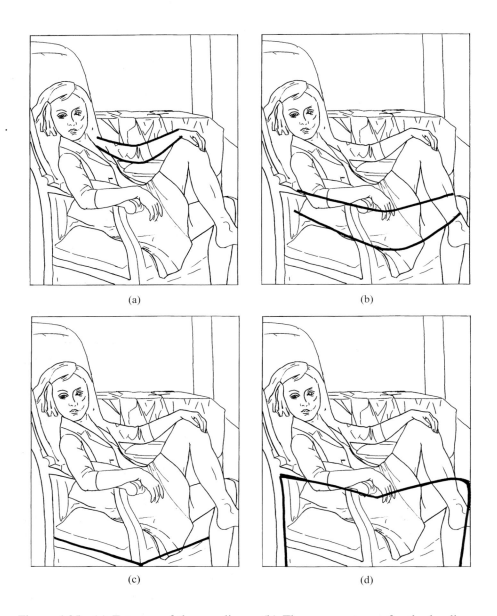

Figure 4.25: (a) Extrema of the arm-lines. (b) The same extrema for the leg-lines. (c) Smoothness-breaking at the bottom of the painting. (d) Stabilization via vertical leg-lines.

The vertexes so far have been downward. However, the next stage in the evolution of the extremum – cusp-formation – occurs in its most significant example, in the upward direction. It is that shown in Fig 4.26a, given by the inner sides of the knee.

The significance of this particular cusp is enormous, as follows: First, it points upward as a powerful countering action against the downward plunge. We will return to this issue later. Second, it continues as the vertical line above the knee, that rises to the top of the canvas, and balances the upward line of the edge of the chair. Third, there is the crucial factor of the type of cusp involved, as follows:

The reader will recall that there are two types of cusp, by virtue of their past history: One comes from a penetrative extremum, and the other from a compressive extremum. Each takes on the historical characteristics of their past extremum. Thus the first cusp has an easy, facilitative and elongated quality; and the second is tough and oppositional.

The cusp we are examining, having arisen from a penetrative extremum, has the first set of characteristics. This is emotionally crucial to the painting. It visually captures the sexual ease, the languid openness to experience, being communicated in the work.

Another significant cusp in the work is entirely implied, but is nevertheless strongly set up by the surrounding structure. It is the cusp into her vagina, as shown in Fig 4.26b. This is established by the lines in her leg – for example, the upper line of the cusp is a symmetry axis. Furthermore, the end of the cusp (at her vagina) is strongly marked by the knob of the chair.

Recall the crucial effect of a cusp: Fig 4.27b shows the preceding stage, the corner. Here, the outward curve manages to resist this movement inward. The next stage is the cusp Fig 4.27c. Here the resistance collapses and the curve caves into the knife.

In the painting by Balthus, this has a clear sexual meaning – communicating the yielding of the girl. Thus, for instance, Balthus uses cusps repeatedly throughout the work, particularly where he pulls long lines together. Consider for example, the lines that flow into her jacket, as shown in Fig 4.28a. Or again, the wonderful fluted outline of her skirt, as shown in Fig 4.28b. Such systems of converging lines are used even within the skirt, as extended converging creases – shown in Fig 4.28c and Fig 4.28d.

Next consider the opposition between the upward and downward forces. As was seen, the knee acts as an upward force in opposition to the downward force of the central plunge. The upward action of the knee is imitated on the left by the upward action of the head as shown in Fig 4.29a.

The crucial thing to observe is that the three curvature extrema – the head, the central plunge, and the knee – form a continuous line, as can be seen in Fig 4.29a. The consequence is that the three inferred process-arrows are seen as having caused the line to oscillate. This introduces not only the crucial theme of oscillation in the painting, but another theme that is even more important, as follows:

Observe that the particular oscillation just described consists of two upward extrema with a downward one in between. The visual effect is that the downward one appears to be *suspended* between the two upward ones – somewhat like a hammock suspended between two posts. This is crucial in giving the sense of slumped, compliant, laziness to the body.

The theme of suspension is used a number of times to structure the body. For example, recall that we observed that the arm at the center of the painting is imitated by

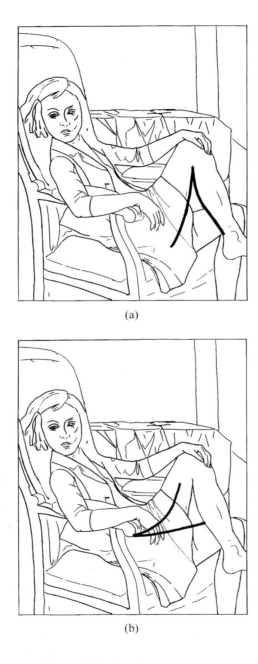

(a)

(b)

Figure 4.26: Two important cusps.

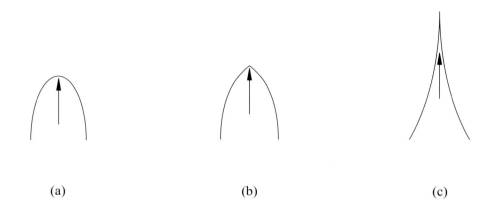

(a)   (b)   (c)

Figure 4.27: The three-stage scenario.

the lower of the two legs. What should be noted now is that both the arm and the lower leg are suspensions: As shown in Fig 4.29b, the arm is suspended, at one end, over the extremum of the upper knee, and, at the other end, over the extremum of the shoulder. Similarly, the imitated structure below is suspended, at one end, over the extremum at the lower knee, and, at the other end, over the extremum where the chair-arm meets the chair-leg.

It will now be seen that the theme of suspension, carried by curvature extrema, invades most of the structures of the painting, and is often combined with the cusping effect to add to the sense of languid compliance.

Consider, for example, the shape shown in Fig 4.29c. Most importantly, the reader should view this shape in the actual photograph, Plate 10. Here, a number of things can be observed: First, the shape is at the center of the painting. This anchors it as the single most important individual shape in the work. Observe that our eye is constantly lead into it, and having entered it, we receive a key to the painting, as follows: The shape captures the main structural themes we have been discussing so far. First, it contains the effect of the central plunge in both its upper lower lines. Second, it contains the sense of suspension – indeed, the shape, *as a whole*, seems to be suspended from its two ends. Third, we have the smoothness-breaking at the two ends. The right end, in particular, is close to becoming a cusp.

Observe now that this shape can be regarded as a bent triangle. Triangles are extremely significant in the work. The most prominent is that formed by the raised knee in relation to the horizontal portion of leg below it. Because of the importance of this large structure, Balthus takes the triangle and uses it repeatedly throughout the work, exploring its distortions. Fig 4.29d shows some of them. What is evident is that Balthus

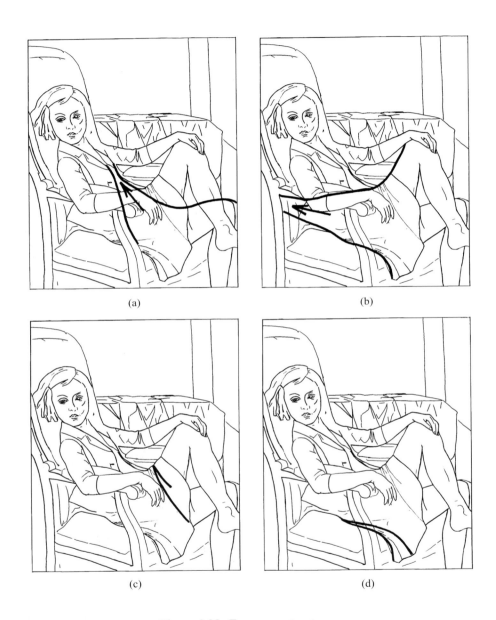

Figure 4.28: Four cusp structures.

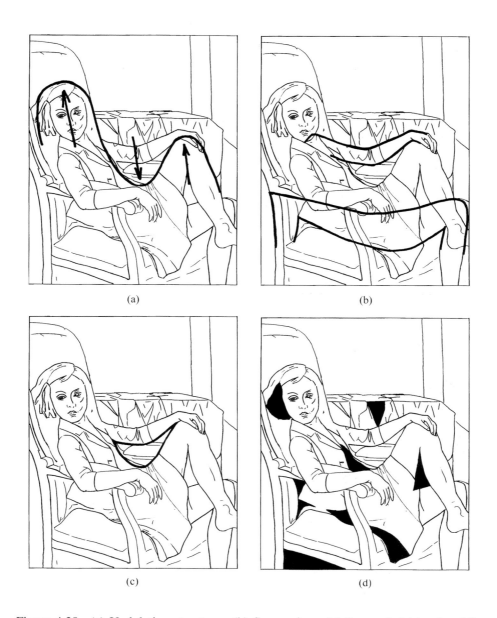

(a)　　　　　　　　　　　　　　　(b)

(c)　　　　　　　　　　　　　　　(d)

Figure 4.29: (a) Undulation structure. (b) Suspension. (c) Suspended triangle. (d) Triangle structures.

exploits the fact that the three vertices of a triangle point in three different directions. In this way, he uses the triangles to set up a sinuous mass of contrary directions across the canvas – communicating very much the sensuous manipulation of flesh and desire.

Now observe the following phenomenon: Consider the triangle in Fig 4.30a, and, in particular, consider the upper vertex. It is, of course, a curvature extremum, and, by our rules, it has a symmetry axis leading to it. Next insert a knife along the axis, such that the knife points toward the extremum. Finally, drag the knife along the axis so that it pushes on the extremum. The vertex changes into a cusp, as shown in Fig 4.30b. This is, of course, our familiar cusp-formation operation. It can be used on one or more of the vertices of the triangle. Clearly, Balthus employs this operation in several of the triangles of the painting.

In fact, Balthus uses the operation also on the rectangle, which is the other significant polygon of the painting. This derives from the canvas shape itself – an issue we shall analyze in detail in this series of books. Consider the large rectangle that occupies the entire region above the table. Its outline is shown in Fig 4.31. One sees that the cusp-formation operation has been applied to its top left vertex. The implied end-point is off the left edge of the canvas.

Balthus applies the operation often to two or more of the corners of other rectangles in the painting. For example, consider the beautiful shape formed by the shadow in Fig 4.32a. It is worthwhile finding this in the actual painting, Plate 10, because Balthus emphasizes the cusps by subtly elongating them, as shadows, onto the positive objects such as the leg.

Observe the way that the artist carries out this theme endlessly. Thus directly above this area, there is the shadow over the leg as shown by the shaded area in Fig 4.32b. This too uses the cusp operation. Again, the reader should find this shadow in the actual painting, in order to fully appreciate it. It is clear that Balthus means us to see this shadow on the leg itself, both as a separate shape in its own right, and fused together with the shape below it as a single unified whole. The unified shape is shown in Fig 4.32c, and it is of extraordinary beauty.

Again, this unified shape is itself united with the shape below it to produce the entire shape shown in Fig 4.32d.

The wonderful beauty of these shapes attests to the fact that Balthus turns each shape into a work of art in its own right. They can stand alone as exquisitely worked-out organizations of tension that carry the expressive meaning of the painting. And furthermore, each, when united with its adjoining shapes, carries the same high level of organizational and expressive power.

The shapes we have just been examining, in Fig 4.32a-d, are mainly negative ones – i.e., background organizations that arise in the world accidentally between the foreground figures. And yet Balthus turns each into a masterpiece of structure and expression. Indeed, it is perhaps the case that no one in the history of art has been more gifted than Balthus in the creation and use of negative shape.

It is worth looking finally at the way Balthus elaborates his structural themes in the minute details of the work. First consider Fig 4.33. It shows two cusps that rise within the upper arm, from the elbow. The reader should now look at them in the painting itself, Plate 10, to fully appreciate them, and see that they are in fact shadows.

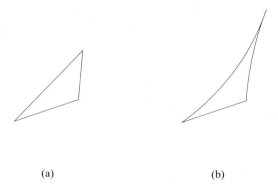

(a)   (b)

Figure 4.30: Cusping of a vertex in a triangle.

Figure 4.31: The cusping of a vertex in a rectangle.

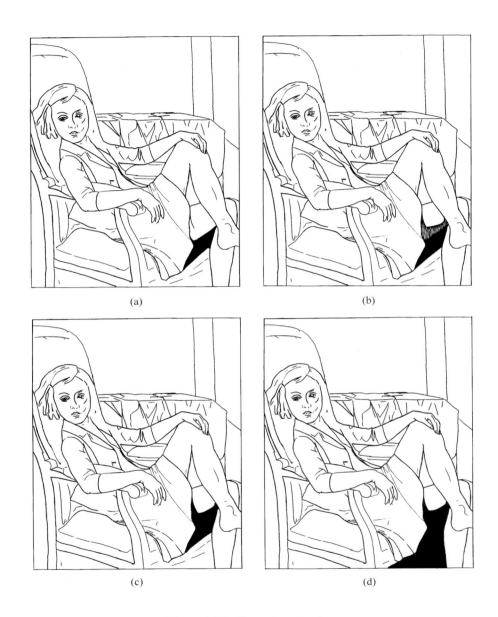

(a)   (b)

(c)   (d)

Figure 4.32: Cusped rectangles.

Figure 4.33: The cusp-theme in the arm.

Now observe that, because they point in the upward direction, they oppose the direction of the downward central plunge. Thus they reinforce the theme of upward/downward opposition described earlier. Furthermore, observe that they actually rise from the central point of the painting.

Next let us consider the white table-cloth. Observe the beautiful complex of creases that make up the cloth. Each of the structural themes we have been discussing is used in this. For example, the central shadow of the cloth is a downward pointing cusp, as the reader can see directly from the painting, Plate 10. This reinforces the theme of upward/downward opposition described earlier. Again, the other shadows form upward and downward pointing triangles. Furthermore, the cloth is constructed also as a sequence of rectangles, as shown in Fig 4.34a - thus reinforcing the rectangle theme.

Finally, Fig 4.34b shows the entire shape of the cloth. One can see that this imitates the shape of the hand below it.

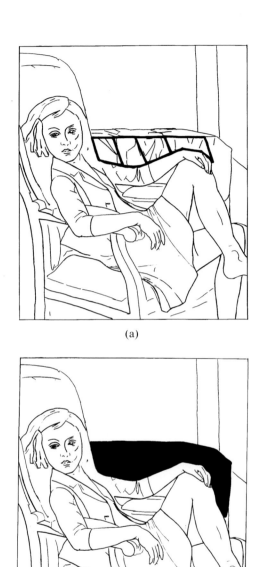

(a)

(b)

Figure 4.34: Table-cloth structures.

Figure 4.35: A major arc.

4.10 Balthus: *Thérèse Dreaming*

The second of the Thérèse paintings will now be examined. It is given as color Plate 11.

Although there are stylistic similarities between this work and the previous one, it is structurally different. The canvas is divided strongly into two halves by the central vertical line that descends through her elbow and emerges as the chair-leg below. The girl is confined mainly to the right half of the canvas, and can be seen as a complete shape, surrounded by space – a shape that will now be studied in detail.

The first thing to observe about this shape is that, whereas in the previous painting the body involved a prominent vertical oscillation, in contrast, in the present painting, the body is mainly constructed as a horizontal oscillation, as will soon be seen. This does not mean that there are not some vertical movements – for example, the raised knee occurs as it did in the previous work. However, these examples are now isolated – they are used to disrupt, to puncture, other structures. In contrast the horizontal movements are unified into oscillating lines that swing backwards and forwards down the painting in beautifully drawn rhythms. These movements will now be considered. They are created by curvature extrema.

First, and most obviously, as shown in Fig 4.35, there is the long horizontal axis formed across the two elbows. The elbows are, of course, curvature extrema. The axis is an amalgam of the two associated symmetry axes – one for each extremum. The importance of this long axis is further emphasized by the fact that the girl's head is pointing along this line. Therefore, the head is used compositionally in a very different way from the previous painting, where the head stared out at us as a single symmetrical oval. Here, the horizontal directedness of her head and the elbow extrema, help to set up a line that projects across the entire canvas as shown in Fig 4.35. The line is caught by the tops of the vases on the table and is thus slightly bent to give an elastic, spring-like, quality.

Figure 4.36: An inward extremum.

The elbows are outward movements from her body. However, below these, towards her waste, there are inward movements. The strongest one comes from the left, along the table, into her side, as shown in Fig 4.36. The arch of the extremum has been drawn here. Although the tip is not visible in the painting itself (Plate 11), it is strongly implied by the upper and lower sides of the arch, which are prominently visible: The upper side is her arm, and the lower side is her horizontal leg. The reader should turn to the painting itself, Plate 11, to fully appreciate the strength of the arch, and the power of the inward movement that is inferred from it.

At the corresponding position on the other side of her body, there is an inward movement coming from the right. On this side, one sees the extremum structure in full, and sees that it is *bay*. The historical structure of a bay was described fully in pages

58-63, and we do not need to repeat the details here, except to recall that the inward movement, bifurcates. Therefore, in the current shape, the inward movement bifurcates, one branch going to her armpit, and the other going to her waist.

Observe that the bay is imitated in the back of the cat, and also the sides of the vases on the table.

Moving down from the waist, one arrives at the region of the legs. They burst out of, and overlap, the skirt – and it is worth concentrating on the latter for a while. Fig 4.37 shows the outline of the skirt. The reader should find this shape in the painting itself, Plate 11. It is the outer line of the red material of the skirt, and will be referred to simply as the *red outline*.

Observe first that it continues behind each of the legs, and is thus a closed smooth shape. Pages 25-26 gave a systematic catalogue of all closed smooth shapes with up to eight extrema. The shape, being considered now, occurs as the second one with six extrema, in that catalogue, and is shown again here in Fig 4.38. The reader merely has to rotate it to arrive at the shape in the painting.

Before considering Fig 4.38 more fully, let us return to Plate 11, and look at this shape. As as ones eye moves around its outline, one is aware of the subtly changing tension. The advantage of finding this shape in the catalogue is that one can fully understand and map out this subtlety of tension. The reason is that our rules identify and label the curvature extrema on a shape, and infer the associated process-arrows. It is this information that corresponds to the tension structure and the expressive quality of the shape.

Let us see how valuable this information is. Return to the painting itself (Plate 11). At first, our attention is caught by the downward plunge of the red skirt, and the leftward direction of the knee. These are the two M^+ extrema at the top of Fig 4.38. However, Fig 4.38 tells us that much more is going on, as follows:

At either side of Fig 4.38, there are two m^+ extrema, where the curve is the flattest. Although these catch the attention much less than the two M^+ extrema, they are just as important a part of the expressive structure of the shape: Observe that one of the m^+ extrema is the flat right side of the red skirt, and the other is its flat top side that is visible above the horizontal thigh. If the reader concentrates on these two flat regions, it will soon become obvious that these two extrema have a crucial expressive role within the shape. This role is given precisely by the six historical characteristics of a m^+ extremum:

compressive flattening broadening oppositional inward squashing.

This contrasts with the six historical characteristics for a M^+ extremum:

penetrative sharpening tightening facilitative outward protrusion.

Thus one can go around this shape and precisely define its tension structure. In fact, since the curve has six extrema, there are six times six (thirty-six) historical characteristics distributed around it. Each is precisely defined.

Now turn to the issue of smoothness-breaking. For this, first go back to the extrema at the elbows, and specifically concentrate on the inner line of the arms – which forms the shape seen in Fig 4.39. This should be found in the painting itself (Plate 11), and fully

Figure 4.37: The outline of the skirt.

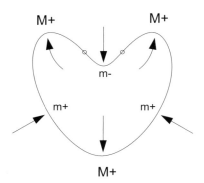

Figure 4.38: One of the shapes from the classification on p25-26.

Figure 4.39: A pointed ellipse.

appreciated. Observe that the extrema are very sharp, and the shape therefore forms a pointed ellipse – which is a structure discussed previously in *Demoiselles d'Avignon*. It was observed, in that discussion, that such an ellipse is created as a result of applying the smoothness-breaking operation to the two penetrative extrema at either end of a *smooth* ellipse.

The pointed ellipse in the arms is repeated very subtly a number of times in the painting. To see this, observe first that the shape of the elbow on the right is imitated exactly by the green cushion below. Now locate the shadow-line that goes from the girl's upper knee to the table. This continues the upper line of the green cushion, as can be appreciated in Fig 4.40a. One can see therefore that Balthus is suggesting here the same pointed ellipse shape as the arm structure above it.

As another example, consider the cloth that hangs from the table at the left. Each of the lines in it has an important structural role in the painting. Consider, in particular, the two unbroken lines that have been indicated on the cloth in Fig 4.40b. The reader should find these in the painting itself (Plate 11), and see that they are indeed strongly highlighted. As can be seen from Fig 4.40b, the upper one continues the line in her arms, and the lower one points towards her vaginal region. Together, the lines form the left side of a pointed ellipse. The right side is shown in Fig 4.40c.

Several more examples are hinted at, in the background. For instance, the lower

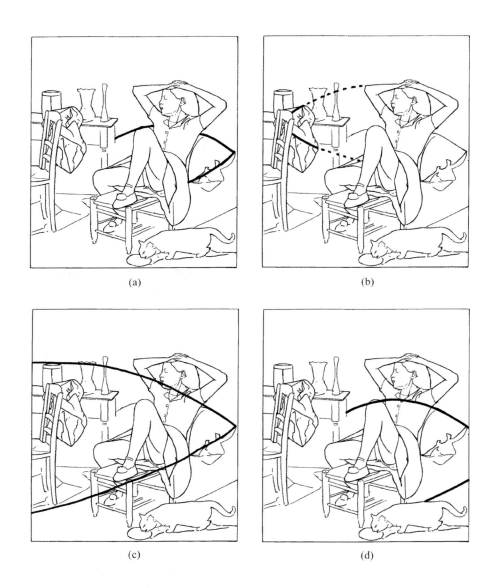

Figure 4.40: Pointed ellipses.

bold line in Fig 4.40d shows a prominent shadow line – which the reader should find in the painting (Plate 11). This complements the upper line shown in Fig 4.40d, and again suggests a pointed ellipse.

Now, the pointed ellipse is taken to a further stage of development: it becomes a diamond. This transition occurred also in *Demoiselles d'Avignon*, where it was fully analyzed. There is no reason to repeat this analysis here (the transition is rigorously given by the Fifth Evolution Law and the smoothness-breaking operation).

Thus the pointed ellipse in the arms changes into a number of diamonds in the painting. The most prominent is the seat of the chair – emphasized strongly because the foot rests firmly on it. The next most prominent is vertically oriented: It is the bright white cloth hanging at the right side of her upward thigh.

The smoothness-breaking operation is then taken to the final stage: cusp-formation. The most significant example of this is the upward-pointing cusp below the knee, as shown in Fig 4.41. Also shown in this figure is another cusp, just to the right of this, created by the clothing pulled along the horizontal thigh.

Let us now turn to another issue related to extrema. We saw that the previous Thérèse painting rests on an extremum at the bottom of the painting. Balthus chooses a similar devise here but uses it for an additional purpose: First, like the last painting, the extremum on which the painting rests comes from the chair. In the present case, it is given by the bottom of the central chair-leg, as shown in Fig 4.42. The left line connects the bottom points of three chair-legs, including that of the other chair. The right line is mainly the strong shadow line, which the reader should find in the painting (Plate 11).

The symmetry axis of this large bottom extremum (Fig 4.42) is the central vertical line which was mentioned before – that comes down through her elbow and emerges below as the central chair-leg. This axis is given a real power by the strong, almost defiant stamp of the central foot.

Now, the importance of this bottom extremum is emphasized still further by the bright saucer below it, from which the cat is drinking, and it is to this that we now turn. What should be observed is the following: Not only does the painting sit heavily on this bottom extremum, but the converse also occurs: The girl's body appears to flower upward out of the saucer like a fountain surging from its source. Fig 4.43 shows this effect with three of the significant lines involved: The central one goes along the axis of her body, and culminates at the extremum defined by her head – to be discussed soon. The left line surges upward to the extremum of the knee, and the right one follows the edge of her body.

This upward surge is countered by the downward movements inferred from the pointed ellipses, as will now be illustrated with the arm-structure: Observe that the hands are slightly curved upward, in yielding to the upward pushing action of the head. Most importantly, the head is an upward penetrative extremum, as shown in Fig 4.44 – where the line shown follows the edge of her hair and torso on one side, and follows her profile and torso on the other side. In contrast to this penetrative extremum, the arm-structure implies an ellipse with the strong compressive downward force. The reader should take a while to fully appreciate, in Fig 4.44, the contrasting effect between the arm-ellipse and the particular upward extremum that has been drawn there.

Finally, as with the previous painting, consider Balthus's use of negative space,

Figure 4.41: Cusp-formation.

Figure 4.42: The supporting extremum.

Figure 4.43: Upward surge.

Figure 4.44: Oval.

Figure 4.45: An extraordinary shape constructed in negative space.

which, as was said before, is probably unequalled in the history of art. Fig 4.45 shows
one of the negative shapes. It is an extraordinary achievement – and the reader should
find it in the actual painting (Plate 11), to appreciate its remarkable emotional quality. Its
tension is created mainly by its curvature extrema, for example, the large arrow-head at
the bottom, the knees that invade it, the bay on its left side where the cloth intrudes, etc.
It is these extrema that give the shape its emotional quality, and support our Fundamental
Law of Expression, which states that emotional expression is recovered history.

4.11   Ingres: *Princesse de Broglie*

We now turn to the *Princesse de Broglie*, by Ingres, shown in color Plate 12.
     This is a painting that is built almost entirely out of cusps and the history that creates
cusps. The work rises as a series of great arches up to the quiet cusp in the hairline. But
it also plunges down to the cusp shown in Fig 4.46a. It is worth carefully examining
how this cusp is set up. For example, consider its left half. Observe, from the painting,
Plate 12, that this curve starts as the edge of the skirt on the left and then continues as
the intense shadow, above the thumb.

(a)

(b)

Figure 4.46: Downward plunging cusp.

Now consider Fig 4.46b. As can be seen from this figure, the downward plunge of the cusp starts with the penetrative extremum at the chin, continues with the extremum at the cleavage in her dress, where smoothness is broken, and culminates finally at the hands.

Now consider the edge of the body. An upward series of cusps is used to define the wonderful left line of her body, as can be seen in Fig 4.47a. This figure shows the two major cusps of this line. However, there are other more subtle cusps in the line – for example, at the shoulder, there are several cusps on different microscopic levels, as can be seen directly from the painting (Plate 12).

The right edge of her body is also formed from cusps. Fig 4.47b also shows the major lower cusp at the elbow, and a finer cusp at the shoulder. In addition, the two subtle cusps are shown that define the ends of the cheek.

In this figure, a gap has been left in the heavy line down the right side of her body – a gap over the region of her neck. How does this line continue over the gap? The answer is remarkable and shows Ingres' greatness in carrying his compositional intent into every aspect of the work. The reader should turn to the actual painting, Plate 12, and consider the shadow that Ingres places over the skin in that region. One sees that the edge of the shadow forms a cusp on the skin as shown in Fig 4.47c. This cusp is actually the true visual edge of the skin because the shadow area itself is same color as the wall behind and thus forms a unity with the latter rather than the skin.

The use of shadow in this work is remarkable. Despite the immensely subtle gradation of light, every shadow has a definite shape that participates crucially in the composition. In fact, the shadows set up *flows* across the skin. This is particularly evident in the extraordinary structure of movement across the face. Let us map this out:

Begin with the hair, next to the face, which is important in defining directions with respect to which the movements act. The hair is in two black pieces, left and right, each with approximately the same shape. Thus the extrema in the hair are paired, left and right. There is a pair of upward extrema at the top of the hair, as shown in Fig 4.48a, and a pair of downward extrema at the bottom of the hair, as shown in Fig 4.48b. As will be seen, paired extrema are a basic theme throughout the painting.

Now let us go into the face itself: Consider the forehead. At the top is the central upward cusp. However, against this, one has the downward pull of the pair of extrema shown in Fig 4.48c. It is particularly important that the reader observe the effect of these two extrema in the actual painting, Plate 12. Note how they are seen as pulling down together with the two downward extrema in the hair, and against the two upward extrema in the hair.

Now consider the eye-lids. Fig 4.49a shows the exact shape of the lid of the left eye (viewer's left). The reader can check in the painting that Ingres does indeed define this shape completely – and he does so by setting it against the surrounding shadow. Observe that the shape has an extremum at each end that is curved downward. The two arrows shown therefore imitate and reinforce the pair of downward arrows that have just been seen in the forehead. Exactly the same structure exists for the right eye as can be seen by carefully examining the shadows in the painting.

Next consider the darkened skin area under the eye. This is shown for the left eye in Fig 4.49b. It is the inverse of the upper eye-lid. The reader should examine

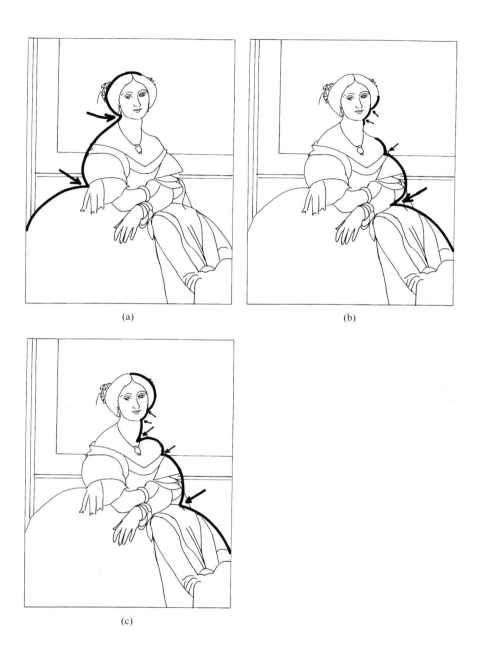

(a)

(b)

(c)

Figure 4.47: Cusps on the side of the body.

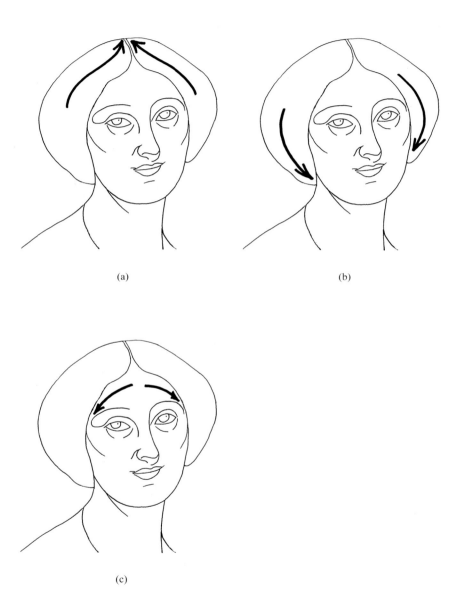

Figure 4.48: Extrema in the hair and forehead.

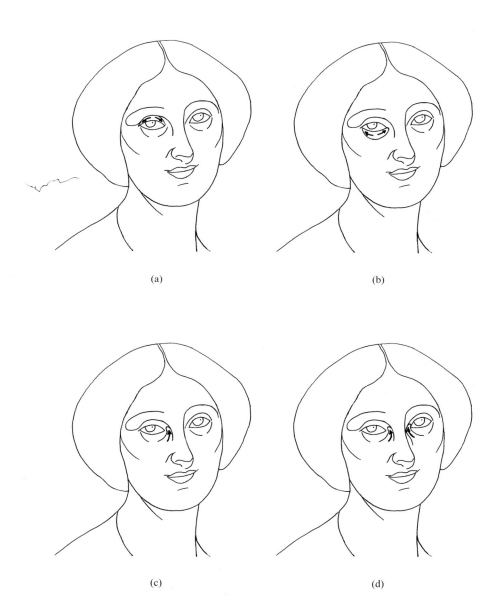

(a)

(b)

(c)

(d)

Figure 4.49: Extrema in the eye-lids.

the painting carefully and see that, indeed, Ingres paints this as a *closed* shape and, in particular, accentuates the extrema at each end. These two extrema define the two directions shown in Fig 4.49b. They are upward and oppose the downward flow in the sides of the forehead.

Now consider the area defined by the arrow in Fig 4.49c. This is a horn-shaped region of light that Ingres again carefully and clearly defines. The reader should again find this area in the actual painting, Plate 12, to see just how clearly it is demarcated. Observe the upward movement created by its arrow – that shown in Fig 4.49c.

The corresponding area by the right eye is even more exquisitely shaped as can be seen directly from the painting, Plate 12. The two shapes define two upward extrema with the inferred arrows shown in Fig 4.49d.

Now consider the two dark shadows above the eyes. Their shapes are shown in Fig 4.50. Again the reader can see how carefully the artist marks the boundaries of these with explicit shadow-lines. Their extrema produce the arrows shown in Fig 4.50.

Let us consider Fig 4.51, which shows an arrow going into a cusp. The cusp is actually a shadow under the cheek – and the reader can easily find this in the painting. The arrow in Fig 4.51 is, of course, the process-history inferred from this cusp. It is directed upwards. A corresponding structure occurs at the cheek on the right side of the face where the cusp is slightly thinner.

The crucial point to observe now is that the movements on the face combine to form a flow. For example, Fig 4.52a shows some of the arrows given so far for the left side of the face. One can see that they create a rotational flow around the eye. The same occurs around the right eye, as shown in Fig 4.52b.

The lower half of the face also involves a complex flow created by cusps. Fig 4.53a shows the cusp of light into the nose, very clearly identifiable on the actual painting, Plate 12. Similarly, there is a cusp of light into the side of the lip as shown in Fig 4.53b. Fig 4.53c shows a strong cusp into the shadows on the chin. Combining these three cusps gives the flow shown in Fig 4.53d.

Exactly the same flow exists on the right half of the face; i.e., into the nose, the lip, and the chin. The reader should take a moment to find and appreciate this structure.

Let us leave the face now and go into the neck. Something seen immediately from Fig 4.54a, is that there are two cusps in the neck, as shown at the bottom of this figure. The reader can check in the painting that these cusps are formed by the necklace meeting the outline of her body. These two cusps are a matched pair on her left and right side.

We can see however that there is a higher additional cusp on the left side of the neck, shown in Fig 4.54b. This is the boundary of a prominent area of light. The reader should identify this in the painting, Plate 12, and observe its importance. For example, it echoes the upward cusp of light at the top of her forehead.

Fig 4.54c shows the flow that is created by the several cusps in this region.

The lowest cusp on the left in Fig 4.54c is part of a movement across the upper chest, shown in Fig 4.55a. In this figure, the bold line that surrounds the arrows is given by the outline of her shoulder, the edge of the necklace, and the edge of her dress. This beautiful shape contains two cusps. From these, one infers the arrows shown. The shape is actually produced by our Third Evolution Law – called shield-formation – which has the same structure as bay-formation except that foreground and background are reversed.

Figure 4.50: Extrema in the eye shadows.

Figure 4.51: Extremum in the cheek shadow.

(a)

(b)

Figure 4.52: Flows on the face.

(a)

(b)

(c)

(d)

Figure 4.53: Setting up a flow in the mouth region.

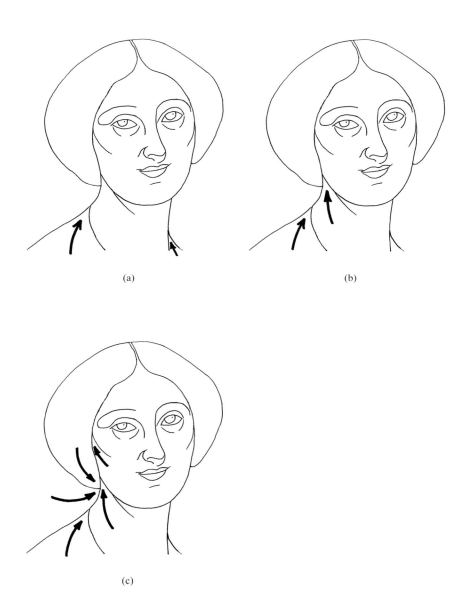

(a)   (b)

(c)

Figure 4.54: Flow in the shoulder and neck.

(a)

(b)

Figure 4.55: Flow in the shoulder and arm.

Figure 4.56: Flows in the sleeve.

Figure 4.57: Downward cusps in negative space.

In the creation of this shape, the use of the Third Evolution Law is then followed by smoothness-breaking and then cusp-formation

Now observe that the lower cusp in this shape matches the lower cusp in the sleeve, as shown in Fig 4.55b. This is an example of the way in which Ingres ties together the different regions of the painting, i.e., by using similar flow factors.

Continuing downward, Fig 4.56 shows the flows created by the edges of the sleeve material, on both the left and right side.

Since enough detail has now been given to show how the flows are set up in a region, we can leave it to the reader to continue downward through the painting and map out the lower flows. Besides the lines in the clothing, it is most important to observe the shapes of the shadows. These crucially participate in the structure of movement, but can easily overlooked.

One final comment should be made. It has been seen throughout the above discussion that Ingres tends to match extrema, left and right, in pairs – both members of a pair pointing in the same direction, either up or down. Examples of this have been seen in the hair, the forehead, etc. All of these examples were, in fact, of positive space. It is therefore useful to finish with a major example in negative space, shown in Fig 4.57. These two downward cusps, made with the edge of the painting, are so large that they interact with each of the cusp pairs which have been discussed so far. Over-all, their downward force tends to give the work its sombre, somewhat depressed quality. The woman rises as a series of arches, but this is against the sense of gravity created by this large downward movement.

4.12   Modigliani: *Jeanne Hébuterne*

In our study of smoothness-breaking, let us look finally at one of Modigliani's portraits of Jeanne Hébuterne, shown in Plate 13.

The biographical background is this: Jeanne was the remarkable, strong-minded, artistically-gifted, woman, with whom Modigliani lived in the last two and a half years of his life – till his death at age 35. She had left her comfortable home to live with the artist in his poverty and rejection by society – and she had done so against the strong opposition of her family. When Modigliani died, on a Saturday night in January 1920, she returned home to her family, and, at dawn on the Monday morning, threw herself out of the fifth-floor window to her death. Here, in this portrait from November 1918, she is pregnant with their daughter. Hardly a year before her death, she is nineteen years old.

Artist and model face each other in the private silent truth of who they are. This moment is scored into the canvas as if it were the stone that Modigliani used to carve – for sculpture was his main artistic expression until he was forced to give it up for health reasons.

Let us see how he constructs the work. Consider Fig 4.58. It shows the fact that the face is an ellipse whose top and bottom ends are penetrative extrema. These emphasize a vertical axis that has been slightly tilted. This theme of tilting is an important one

Figure 4.58: The ellipse with its penetrative extrema.

in the painting. The rotating movement started by the head is carried further almost to the horizontal where it is caught by a sequence of rightward extrema, as follows: First there is the rightward cusp shown in Fig 4.59a – into her neck. The path started by this extremum is extended further by another rightward cusp – into the inner crease of the elbow – as shown in Fig 4.59b. The next extremum on this path is the smoothness-broken extremum at the elbow itself – as shown in Fig 4.59c. This trajectory of rightward arrows is then twisted downward into the final cusp at the right edge of the painting – shown in Fig 4.59d.

This last extremum sets up a circular clockwise movement whose upward movement on the other side of the painting is given by the sharp extremum on the left in Fig 4.60.

In addition, the curved downward movement of the right extremum is repeated in the dress as shown in Fig 4.61a. These two matched downward extrema are then imitated by two matched downward extrema at the bottom of the painting, as shown in Fig 4.61b.

Let us now return to the neck. We have considered the rightward movement across her neck. However there is also a leftward movement across the neck that is quieter but is nevertheless present. It is set up by two virtually identical extrema, as shown in Fig 4.62a. The reader should find these two extrema in the actual painting itself, Plate

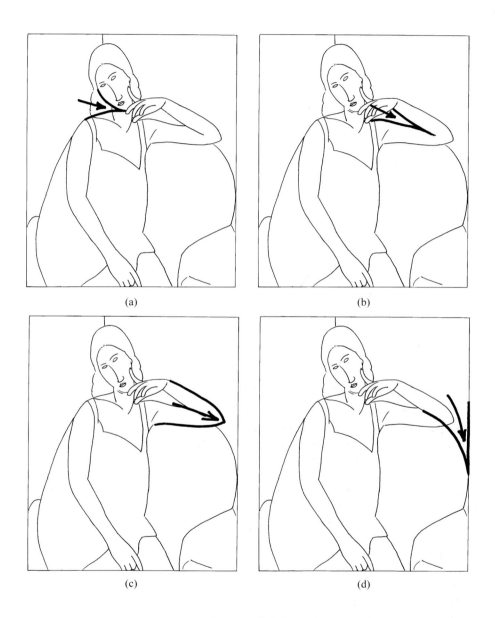

Figure 4.59: Trajectory of rightward extrema.

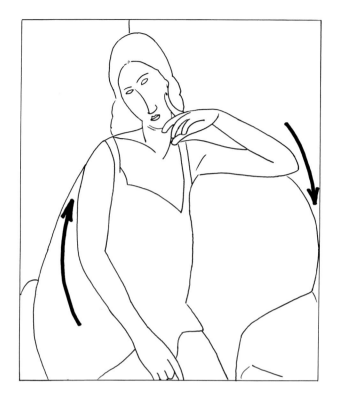

Figure 4.60: Extrema setting up circular movement.

13, and fully appreciate their similarity. They reinforce the theme of matching pairs of extrema that occurs a number times in the painting.

The leftward movement produced by the two extrema just discussed is further emphasized by the two extrema shown in Fig 4.62b, both created by the smoothness-breaking operation, κ.

Note that the neck also involves an additional movement – a downward one, as follows: The downward smooth extremum of the chin sits in a downward cusp, as seen in Fig 4.63a. And below this, is a further downward cusp as shown in Fig 4.63b. One can therefore see that the neck is a crucial node across which movements flow in different directions. All these movements are created by extrema.

Finally observe that another prominent theme in this painting is the strong contrast between penetrative and compressive extrema. This starts in the head: By elongating the ellipse of the head, the artist accentuates the difference between the two penetrative extrema, at the top and bottom of this ellipse, and the two compressive extrema that form the two strongly flattened sides of that ellipse. This contrast – between penetrative and compressive extrema – is one which Modigliani exploits in many of his works including his sculpture. In this painting, there is the powerful compressive extremum that occurs

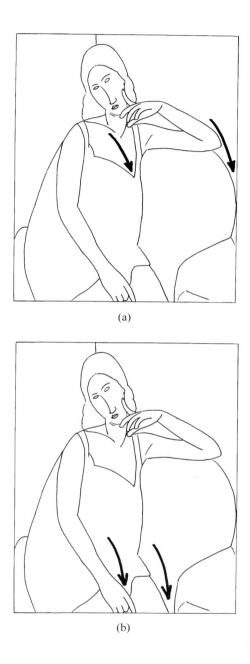

(a)

(b)

Figure 4.61: Pairs of downward extrema.

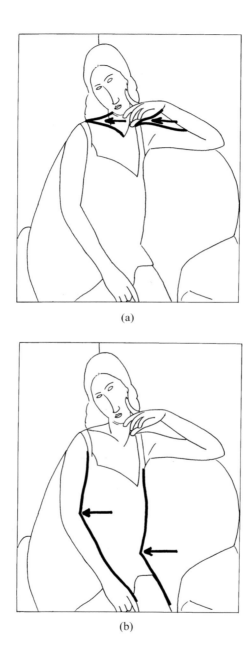

(a)

(b)

Figure 4.62: Pairs of leftward extrema.

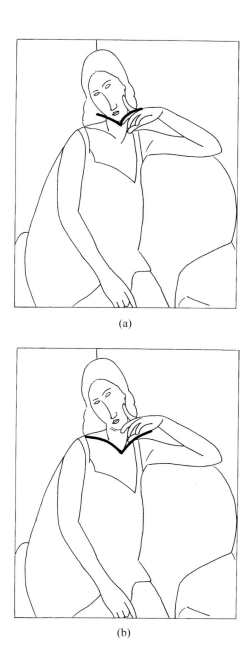

(a)

(b)

Figure 4.63: Downward cusps.

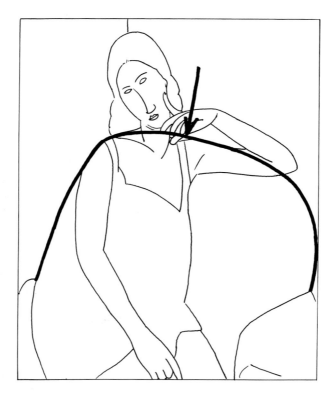

Figure 4.64: Downward compressive extremum.

at the top of the large heavy block that unifies the painting – as shown in Fig 4.64. This vertical compressive force contrasts for example with the vertical penetrative forces in the head.

4.13   The Complete Set of Extrema-Based Rules

The series of paintings, just examined, were used to illustrate the final rule for the extraction of history from curvature extrema, i.e., the Smoothness-Breaking Operator, κ. It is now time to gather the entire set of rules. There are a total of fifteen, and they are shown in Table 4.1, p199. We have seen that each of them serves a powerful role in the visual impact of a painting. Let us examine the table.

Rules 1-3. The first three rules apply to every curvature extremum. For each extremum, the rules produce an arrow along the symmetry axis leading to the extremum. The arrow represents the trajectory that the extremum took in the past to reach its current position. The boundary of the shape is understood as having deformed along the arrow.

These three laws were called the basic laws because none of the others are possible without them.

Rules 4-7. There are four types of extrema. While each receives an arrow showing how the extremum moved to its current state, the four types differ in characteristics of this history, e.g., the trajectory can be outward or inward, etc. Each extremum has six such characteristics. Rules 4-7 are the assignment of these characteristics to the four extrema.

The importance of this assignment is as follows: Our Fundamental Law of Expression states that emotional expression is recovered history. This means that the historical characteristics are the characteristics of the emotional expression of the extrema. Since there are six characteristics of the history, there are therefore six characteristics of the emotional expression.

These are absolutely crucial to the emotional effect of line. Each extremum, on a line, possesses its six characteristics. A great artist is fully aware of them and exploits them. One can literally take a walk around a canvas and see how, at each extremum, the artist has been completely aware of the six historical characteristics of that extremum, and has fully exploited the expressive value of each characteristic. Not a single characteristic can be ignored because it is there, whether the artist likes it or not; and a bad artist is one who is not sensitive to its presence, or cannot use it.

Rule 8. One of the basic requirements of a work of art is unity across positive and negative space. In order to establish this, one has to relate positive to negative *shapes*. This requires the Duality Operator, which converts positive into negative, and vice versa. Rule 8 shows the effect of the operator on the extrema involved. We also studied its effect on the historical characteristics of the individual extrema. It was seen that this is crucial to understanding what happens to the emotional content of a shape in going from its positive to negative version.

Rules 9-14. These six rules are the Evolution Laws of the Process-Grammar. They are, in a sense, the deepest part of our theory of curvature extrema. In fact, they are elaborations of Rule 3 above, as follows:

Rule 3 is a particular example of the Asymmetry Principle. The general statement of this principle is that an asymmetry in the present goes back to a symmetry in the past. In the present case, the asymmetry is distinguishability in curvature – a distinguishability represented by the extrema. The Asymmetry Principle implies that the extrema in the present shape are removed backward in time, leaving a past shape without extrema (this is a circle, if the present shape is smooth). Therefore, going forward in time, the principle says that the past began as a shape without extrema, and the history gradually introduced the extrema, until the present shape was obtained.

Rules 9-14, the Six Evolution Laws of the Process-Grammar, give a detailed map of the emergence of these extrema. Because Rules 1-3 give the history as a single overall phase, they do not define the order in which the extrema appeared. However,

Rules 9-14 decompose the history into an ordered sequence of steps, each of which is an asymmetry-creating event at an extremum. One can say that the Evolution Laws give the building blocks of the history.

Rule 15. The final rule is smoothness-breaking, which converts a smooth extremum into a non-smooth one. A smooth extremum has finite curvature and a non-smooth one has infinite curvature. Thus the Smoothness-Breaking Operator, κ, pushes finite curvature to infinity.

4.14   Final Comments

We saw in Chapter 1 that the new foundations for geometry, elaborated in my books, are entirely opposite to the standard foundations to geometry from Euclid to modern physics including Einstein. Whereas, in the standard foundations, a geometric object is an invariant to applied action (i.e., *memoryless*), in my new foundations, a geometric object is a *memory store* for applied action. A basic principle of the new foundations is that *artworks are maximal memory stores*. Using the new foundations, it now becomes possible to give a complete systematic elaboration of the laws of artistic composition. This is because, according to the new foundations, the laws of artistic composition are the laws of memory storage. These laws are elaborated by the new foundations. The laws take different features of a painting and show how they act as different sources from which memory of past action is extracted. In this volume, we looked at one of these sources, curvature extrema. In the next volume, we will examine other sources in a painting. For this it will be necessary to look at the concept of symmetry more deeply. The purpose of this entire series of volumes is to give a systematic elaboration of all the memory sources in a painting, and therefore to fully define the artwork. The reader who wishes, in addition, to read a full conceptual exposition of my new foundations to geometry should read my book *Symmetry, Causality, Mind* (MIT Press, 630 pages); and the reader who wishes to read the full mathematical foundations should read my book *A Generative Theory of Shape* (Springer-Verlag, 550 pages).

Table 4.1: **THE EXTREMA-BASED LAWS**

THREE BASIC LAWS

(1) Symmetry-Curvature Duality Theorem. Each curvature extremum has a unique axis leading to, and terminating at, the extremum.

(2) Symmetry Principle applied to symmetry axes (Interaction Principle). Processes are understood as having gone along symmetry axes.

(3) Asymmetry Principle applied to curvature variation. Differences in curvature must be removed backwards in time.

HISTORICAL (EMOTIONAL) CHARACTERISTICS OF EXTREMA

(4)	M^+	penetrative	sharpening	tightening	facilitative	outward	protrusion
(5)	m^-	penetrative	sharpening	tightening	facilitative	inward	indentation
(6)	m^+	compressive	flattening	broadening	oppositional	inward	squashing
(7)	M^-	compressive	flattening	broadening	oppositional	outward	resistance

DUALITY OPERATOR.

(8) $$M^+ \longleftrightarrow m^- \qquad m^+ \longleftrightarrow M^-$$

PROCESS GRAMMAR:

(9)	$Cm^+:$	$m^+ \longrightarrow 0m^-0$	(squashing continues till it indents)
(10)	$CM^-:$	$M^- \longrightarrow 0M^+0$	(resistance continues till it protrudes)
(11)	$BM^+:$	$M^+ \longrightarrow M^+m^+M^+$	(sheild-formation)
(12)	$Bm^-:$	$m^- \longrightarrow m^-M^-m^-$	(bay-formation)
(13)	$Bm^+:$	$m^+ \longrightarrow m^+M^+m^+$	(breaking-through of a protrusion)
(14)	$BM^-:$	$M^- \longrightarrow M^-m^-M^-$	(breaking-through of an indentation)

SMOOTHNESS-BREAKING OPERATOR

(15) $$\kappa : e \longrightarrow e_\kappa$$

Bibliography

[1] Blum, H., (1973). Biological shape and visual science. *Journal of Theoretical Biology*, **38**, 205-287.

[2] Brady, J.M., (1983). Criteria for representations of shape. In: A.Rosenfeld & J. Beck, editors. *Human and Machine Vision: Vol 1*. Hillsdale, NJ: Erlbaum.

[3] Hayes, P.J., & Leyton, M. (1989) Processes at discontinuities. *International Joint Conference on Artificial Intelligence*. Detroit. p1267-1272.

[4] Hoffman, D.D. & Richards, W.A. (1985). Parts of recognition. *Cognition*, **18**, 65-96.

[5] Larsen, T.W. (1993). Proces grammatik og proces historie for 2D objekter. DAIMI IR-115, Aarhus Univ.Report

[6] Lee, J.P. (1991). *Scientific Visualization with Glyphs and Shape Grammars*. Master's Thesis, School for Visual Arts, New York.

[7] Leyton, M. (1984) Perceptual organization as nested control. *Biological Cybernetics*, **51**, 141-153.

[8] Leyton, M. (1986a) Principles of information structure common to six levels of the human cognitive system. *Information Sciences*, **38**, 1-120. Entire journal issue.

[9] Leyton, M. (1986b) A theory of information structure I: General principles. *Journal of Mathematical Psychology*, **30**, 103-160.

[10] Leyton, M. (1986c) A theory of information structure II: A theory of perceptual organization *Journal of Mathematical Psychology*, **30**, 257-305.

[11] Leyton, M. (1987a) Nested structures of control: An intuitive view. *Computer Vision, Graphics, and Image Processing*, **37**, 20-53.

[12] Leyton, M. (1987b) Symmetry-curvature duality. *Computer Vision, Graphics, and Image Processing*, **38**, 327-341.

[13] Leyton, M. (1987d) A Limitation Theorem for the Differential Prototypification of Shape. *Journal of Mathematical Psychology*, **31**, 307-320.

[14] Leyton, M. (1988) A Process-Grammar for Shape. *Artificial Intelligence*, **34**, 213-247.

[15] Leyton, M. (1989) Inferring Causal-History from Shape. *Cognitive Science,* **13**, 357-387.

[16] Leyton, M. (1992). *Symmetry, Causality, Mind.* Cambridge, Mass: MIT Press.

[17] Leyton, M. (1999) New foundations for perception. In Lepore, E. (Editor). *Invitation to Cognitive Science.* Blackwell, Oxford. p121 - 171.

[18] Leyton, M. (2001). *A Generative Theory of Shape.* Berlin: Springer-Verlag.

[19] Leyton, M. (2006). *Shape as Memory: A Geometric Theory of Architecture.* Zurich: Birkhauser.

[20] Leyton, M. & Hayes, P.J. (1989) Processes at discontinuities. Tech report, Rutgers University.

[21] Milios, E.E. (1989). Shape matching using curvature processes. *Computer Vision, Graphics, and Image Processing*, **47**, 203-226.

[22] Pernot, J-P., Guillet, S., Leon, J-C., Falcidieno, B., & Giannini, F. (2003). Interactive Operators for free form features manipulation. In SIAM conference on CADG, Seattle, 2003.

[23] Pernot, J-P., Guillet, S., Leon, J-C., Falcidieno, B., & Giannini, F. (2005). Un modèle de description de formes gauches et opérateurs de manipulation associeś. Tech report Laboratoire 3S Grenoble and CNR Genova.

[24] Richards, W., Koenderink, J.J., & Hoffman, D.D. (1987). Inferring three-dimensional shapes from two-dimensional silhouettes. *Journal of the Optical Society of America A*, **4**, 1168-1175.

[25] Shemlon, S. (1994). *The Elastic String Model of Non-Rigid Evolving Contours and its Applications in Computer Vision.* PhD Thesis, Rutgers University.

Credits

Plate 9: Pablo Picasso (1881-1973). *Les Demoiselles d'Avignon*, 1907. Oil on canvas, 8' x 7'8". (243.9 x 233.7 cm). Acquired through the Lille P. Bliss Bequest. (333.1939). The Museum of Modern Art, New York, NY, USA. Digital Image ©The Museum of Modern Art / Licensed by SCALA / Art Resource, NY.
©2006 Estate of Pablo Picasso / Artists Rights Society (ARS), New York.

Plate 10: Balthus (French, 1908-2001), *Thérèse*, 1938, Oil on cardboard mounted on wood: H. 39-1/2, W. 32 inches (100.3 x 81.3 cm): The Metropolitan Museum of Art, Bequest of Mr. and Mrs. Allan D. Emil, in honor of William S. Lieberman, 1987. (1987.125.2) Photograph ©1993 The Metropolitan Museum of Art.
©2006 Artists Rights Society (ARS), New York / ADAGP, Paris.

Plate 11: Balthus (French, 1908-2001), *Thérèse Dreaming*, 1938, Oil on canvas: H. 59, W. 51 inches (150 x 130 cm): The Metropolitan Museum of Art, Jacques and Natasha Gelman Collection, 1998. (1999.363.2) Photograph by Malcolm Varon. Photograph ©1988 The Metropolitan Museum of Art.
©2006 Artists Rights Society (ARS), New York / ADAGP, Paris.

Plate 12: Jean-Auguste-Dominique Ingres (French, 1780-1867), *Princesse de Broglie*, 1851-53, Oil on canvas; 47 3/4 x 35 3/4 in. (121.3 x 90.8 cm): The Metropolitan Museum of Art, Robert Lehman Collection, 1975 (1975.1.186) Photograph ©1998 The Metropolitan Museum of Art.

Plate 13: Amedeo Modigliani (Italian, 1884-1920), *Jeanne Hébuterne*, 1919, Oil on canvas: H. 36, W. 28-3/4 inches (91.4 x 73 cm): The Metropolitan Museum of Art, Gift of Mr. and Mrs. Nate B. Spingold, 1956 (56.184.2) Photograph ©1985 The Metropolitan Museum of Art.

Index

Color Plates

Picasso: Large Still-Life w/ a Pedestal Table

Plate 1

Raphael! Alba Madonna

Plate 2

Cezanne: Italian Girl
Resting on her Elbow

Plate 3

de Kooning! Black Painting Plate 4

Plate 6

Holbein! Anne of Cleves

Plate 7

Gauguin: Vision after
the sermon

Hans Memling: Portrait of a Man

Plate 8

Plate 9

Plate 10

Plate 11

Ingres: Princesse de Broglie

Plate 12

Modigliani?
Jeanne Hebuterne

Plate 13

Springer and the Environment

WE AT SPRINGER FIRMLY BELIEVE THAT AN INTER-national science publisher has a special obligation to the environment, and our corporate policies consistently reflect this conviction.

WE ALSO EXPECT OUR BUSINESS PARTNERS – PRINTERS, paper mills, packaging manufacturers, etc. – to commit themselves to using environmentally friendly materials and production processes.

THE PAPER IN THIS BOOK IS MADE FROM NO-CHLORINE pulp and is acid free, in conformance with international standards for paper permanency.